PUBLICATIONS FOI

Thanks to dialectical and historical materialism, Marx and Engels placed at the disposal of the human race the possibility of extending their scientific method to the analysis of history and society. This is already an extremely important result; but Marxist science is much more than that. Applied to human society, Marxist science explains the processes that make communism a historical necessity, allows the scientific definition of the strategy for the communist revolution, and ensures the superiority of the proletariat over the other classes, a superiority ensured solely by this scientific strategy.

All the Marxist literary works are born as weapons in the revolutionary battle for communism and are only able to survive as such. In one and a half centuries, the fighting of numerous generations of Marxists has led to the accumulation of a scientific patrimony that unfortunately is little known and even less used today.

Arrigo Cervetto, who considered science as the salient feature of Lenin's party and founded his attempt to transfer the Bolshevik experience from tsarist Russia to post-WWII imperialist Italy on this hypothesis, defined the patrimony of Marxist science as a largely unexplored lode.

To bring a part of this theoretical treasure trove back into the light for the English-speaking reader is one of the tasks our publishing house has set itself, not with the aim of spreading culture but with the aim of providing the theoretical weapons with which to fight the revolutionary battle for communism.

The reality of this 21st century as a whole reveals how much of scientifically-founded revolutionary strategy was contained in the final appeal of the "Manifesto" – *Workers of all countries, unite!* An international proletariat that has swollen to huge dimensions has more than ever an urgent need to rediscover Marxist science and, in view of its future battles, to anchor its revolutionary preparation in it.

The work that lies before us is immense. Our catalogue is the measure of the contribution that we, as the Marxist Science publishing house, have succeeded in making so far.

Karl Marx

WAGE LABOUR AND CAPITAL

WAGES, PRICE AND PROFIT

Science
éditions Marxiste

Marxist Science Publications

Publications for young people

For information about our publications please contact
Éditions Science Marxiste S.A.R.L.
10, rue Lavoisier – 93100 Montreuil-sous-Bois, France
E-mail : escmrx@wanadoo.fr – Fax: (+33) 01 49 88 79 82
http ://www.sciencemarxiste.com

ISBN 978-2-490073-02-3

Publisher's note

The present edition is based on the texts contained in Marx-Engels Collected Works, Volumes 9, 20 and 27, International Publishers, 1977, 1985 and 1990, respectively. The publisher is available for contact by anyone claiming translation rights.

Contents

Editor's Note

In the face of the escalating uncertainty and fears generated by the multiplication of the social shocks of globalisation, the confusion and disastrous crisis of bourgeois politics are becoming increasingly evident. An example is its attempt to deal with the growing pressures of the world market, imposing in every country a policy of conciliation of the interests among the classes, behind which to enrol, powerless, each sector of the proletariat.

It is especially at such critical junctures that the need for the clarity of communist and revolutionary science asserts itself even more forcibly... starting from the fixed point of the principle of class distinction and the persistent conflict between capital and wages that continues more than ever to fuel our epoch and its irreconcilable antagonisms.

The two texts we have collected together in this volume were written between 1847 and 1865. But even though they were written one hundred and fifty years ago, and in spite of their conciseness, they have the amazing ability to clarify a number of current problems. Moreover, they are an illustration of Marx's ability to "popularise" complex notions: in fact they present the bases of economic analysis in a way that is both simple and scientific. These two works, *Wage Labour and Capital* and *Wages, Price and Profit*, offer a solid, irreplaceable base for the study of the Marxist theory of economics.

Wage Labour and Capital finds all its richness and modernity in its combination between the aim for which it was written and its key idea. According to the latter, it is the nature of capitalism to conceal relations among people under the appearance of relations among "things". The mysterious characteristics of such "things" as capital or wages can be clarified by tracing them back to their underlying relations, relations among people. What explains the topicality of this text is precisely the fact that the fundamental relation, even today, has not changed. Society is founded on the relation established between the minority of people who monopolise the means of production – capitalists – and the vast majority of those who are without them and who are therefore obliged to sell their capacity to work – wage earners.

The effects of imperialist maturation on the social strata are not dealt with in this study because that maturation had not yet taken place at the time. However, Marx was far from the caricatural pauperism that is often attributed to him. The law he formulates here about the tendency of wages to decrease does not concern their absolute value; it regards that share of social product corresponding to them. In view of the rapid, capitalism-induced growth in the social product, wages can increase – thus forging what Marx calls "golden chains" – but less than the incomes of the other classes. Regarding this consideration – more than ever topical today – a clarification is required: it is necessary to distinguish between *incomes* and *wages*. The typical family of imperialist maturation has various sources of *income*: more than one wage, with the diffusion of women's employment, wages and incomes, resulting from the access of vast strata of wage workers to property. The main novelty is that this transformation has changed the workers' situation as they face the precariousness of their existence, which has remained unchanged. Precariousness is the result of the law of capitalist development "which again and again throws bourgeois production out of its old course and which compels capital to intensify the productive forces of labour", as Marx explains in the first of these two studies. The *crisis in global relations* shows that the wage earners' situation has not changed much in this regard, even if in the countries that have reached imperialist maturity, incomes and property cushion the blow today. This is one of the reasons for social passivity and the absence of widespread reactions on the part of the proletariat, hard hit by the crisis.

The clarity of exposition, as Engels explains in his introduction, stems from the will to "popularise" economic theory among the workers. In its initial form, *Wage Labour and Capital* was a series of lectures Marx had delivered before the German Workers' Society in Brussels, and then of articles published in the *Neue Rheinische Zeitung.* Marx's intention was not intellectual, but revolutionary. It was not a matter of academic reflection, but of leading a battle. Moreover, parallel to the economic texts collected in this volume, the *Neue Rheinische Zeitung* chronicled the revolution that was underway at the time in Germany and gave the proletariat indications about how to fight.

Wages, Price and Profit had the same aim. Originally, it was a document read by Marx in the course of two sessions of the General Council of the International Workingmen's Association, better known today as the First International. In these addresses, Marx answered the questions raised by the "old Owenite", John Weston, about the impact of the increase in wages on the workers' situation and the position of the trade unions in wage battles.

The Council would have liked to have this text printed. In a letter of June 24, 1865, Marx asked for Engels' advice on the appropriateness of this publication. Among the reasons for his doubts, he recalled that "the second part of the paper contains, in an extraordinarily condensed *but relatively popular form*, many new ideas which are anticipated from my book, whilst at the same time it does, of necessity, have to skate over a lot of problems." Engels replied that he saw no problem in anticipating "a few odd points from your book – N. B. if the latter is *really* almost finished now – how does it stand? The ultimate and final date for completion was 1 September, and the price, you remember, is 12 bottles of wine." What lies behind this anecdote was that the two revolutionaries were speaking about *Capital* and Engels jokingly solicited its long-awaited publication, which would indeed occur in September, but two years later. As for the text of the addresses, Marx and Engels ended up refusing to see it published, with the result that *Wages, Price and Profit* would be published as a booklet only after their deaths.

The "novelties" the leaders of the First International had the chance to know in preview, without really realising it at the time, were none other than the discovery of the "value of labour" or, more precisely, of the fact that it is impossible to determine this value without introducing the concept of "labour-power". *Wages, Price and Profit* thus constitutes the first scientific explanation of the mechanism of capitalist exploitation.

"Citizen Weston" was certainly not of the calibre to vie with Marx, and without their controversy his theses would undoubtedly be totally forgotten today. But the issue went beyond that controversy : it was a matter of orienting the trade union leaders and, in a more general way, the European proletariat in the direction to give to wage struggles, at a moment when the whole continent was prey to "a real epidemic of strikes".

At Marx's time, money was gold or a symbol of gold. It is to that reality, and not to today's fiduciary and fiat money, that his studies referred. In spite of this important difference, the content of his theses is still fully valid. The wage struggle is the objective phenomenon that fixes the price of labour-power and on which, to a certain extent, the workers' living conditions depend. But the workers' liberation cannot stem from the wage struggle : it requires the revolutionary struggle for the abolition of wage labour, i.e. the struggle for Communism.

Lenin made an important distinction between "vulgarisation" and "popularisation". The first notion considers that the reader is incapable of understanding by himself. "In a distortedly simplified form [it] hands out 'ready-made' *all* the conclusions of a known theory, so that the reader does not even have to chew but merely to swallow what he is given." On the contrary, as Lenin wrote in 1901, popularisation assumes "in the undeveloped reader a serious intention to use his head and *aids* him in his serious and difficult work, leads him, helps him over his first steps, and *teaches* him to go forward independently." The effort to popularise, of which the two studies are an example, places them among the masterpieces of Marxist science.

Friedrich Engels

Introduction to the German edition (1891) of *Wage Labour and Capital*

Engels wrote this Introduction for the new separate edition of Marx's work *Wage Labour and Capital*, which appeared in Berlin in 1891 and which he edited. In the opening part of the Introduction Engels reproduced an introductory note he had written for an earlier edition of this work, one that appeared in 1884. The edition containing Engels' Introduction had a large print run in order to promote the circulation of Marx's economic teachings among the workers.

The following work appeared as a series of leading articles in the *Neue Rheinische Zeitung* from April 4, 1849 onwards. It is based on the lectures delivered by Marx in 1847 at the German Workers' Society in Brussels.[a] The work as printed remained a fragment; the words at the end of No. 269: "To be continued," remained unfulfilled in consequence of the events which just then came crowding one after another: the invasion of Hungary by the Russians,[b] the insurrections in Dresden, Iserlohn, Elberfeld, the Palatinate and Baden, which led to the suppression of the newspaper itself (May 19, 1849). The manuscript of the continuation was not found among Marx's papers after his death.[c]

Wage Labour and Capital has appeared in a number of editions as a separate publication in pamphlet form, the last being in 1884, by the Swiss Co-operative Press, Hottingen-Zurich. The editions hitherto published retained the exact wording of the original. The present new edition, however, is to be circulated in not less than 10,000 copies as a propaganda pamphlet, and so the question could not but force itself upon me whether under these circumstances Marx himself would have approved of an unaltered reproduction of the original.

---

[a] The *German Workers' Society in Brussels* was founded by Marx and Engels at the end of August 1847, its aim being to provide a political education for German workers living in Belgium, and to spread the ideas of scientific communism among them. Its activities ceased soon after the February 1848 bourgeois revolution in France, when the Society's members were arrested and banned by the Belgian police. [Ed.]

[b] A reference to the intervention of Russian troops in Hungary in 1849 to suppress the revolution and restore the Habsburg power. [Ed.]

[c] Only some notes entitled "Wage" were found. They were not published in this edition. [Ed.]

In the forties, Marx had not yet finished his critique of political economy. This took place only towards the end of the fifties. Consequently, his works which appeared before the first part of *A Contribution to the Critique of Political Economy* (1859) differ in some points from those written after 1859, and contain expressions and whole sentences which, from the point of view of the later works, appear unfortunate and even incorrect. Now, it is self-evident that in ordinary editions intended for the general public this earlier point of view also has its place, as a part of the intellectual development of the author, and that both author and public have an indisputable right to the unaltered reproduction of these older works. And I should not have dreamed of altering a word of them.

It is another thing when the new edition is intended practically exclusively for propaganda among workers. In such a case Marx would certainly have brought the old presentation dating from 1849 into harmony with his new point of view. And I feel certain of acting as he would have done in undertaking *for this edition* the few alterations and additions which are required in order to attain this object in all essential points. I therefore tell the reader beforehand: this is not the pamphlet as Marx wrote it in 1849 but approximately as he would have written it in 1891. The actual text, moreover, is circulated in so many copies that this will suffice until I am able to reprint it again, unaltered, in a later complete edition.

My alterations [a] all turn on one point. According to the original, the worker sells his *labour* to the capitalist for wages; according to the present text he sells his labour *power*. And for this alteration I owe an explanation. I owe it to the workers in order that they may see it is not a case here of mere juggling with words, but rather of one of the most important points in the whole of political economy. I owe it to the bourgeois, so that they can convince themselves how vastly superior the uneducated workers, for whom one can easily make comprehensible the most difficult

---

[a] The reader will find Marx's original text of 1849 in the footnotes. [Ed.]

economic analyses, are to our supercilious "educated people" to whom such intricate questions remain insoluble their whole life long.

Classical political economy took over from industrial practice the current conception of the manufacturer, that he buys and pays for the *labour* of his workers. This conception had been quite adequate for the business needs, the book-keeping and price calculations of the manufacturer. But, naively transferred to political economy, it produced there really wondrous errors and confusions.

Political economy observes the fact that the prices of all commodities, among them also the price of the commodity that it calls "labour", are continually changing; that they rise and fall as the result of the most varied circumstances, which often bear no relation whatever to the production of the commodities themselves, so that prices seem, as a rule, to be determined by pure chance. As soon, then, as political economy made its appearance as a science, one of its first tasks was to seek the law which was concealed behind this chance apparently governing the prices of commodities, and which, in reality, governed this very chance. Within the prices of commodities, continually fluctuating and oscillating, now upwards and now downwards, political economy sought for the firm central point around which these fluctuations and oscillations turned. In a word, it started from the prices of commodities in order to look for the *value* of the commodities as the law controlling prices, the value by which all fluctuations in price are to be explained and to which finally they are all to be ascribed.

Classical political economy then found that the value of a commodity is determined by the labour contained in it, requisite for its production. With this explanation it contented itself. And we also can pause here for the time being. I will only remind the reader, in order to avoid misunderstandings, that this explanation has nowadays become totally inadequate. Marx was the first thoroughly to investigate the value-creating quality of labour and he discovered in so doing that not all labour apparently, or even really, necessary for the production of a commodity adds to it under all circumstances a magnitude of value which corresponds to the quantity of labour expended. If therefore today we say offhandedly with economists like Ricardo that the value of a commodity is determined by the labour necessary for its production, we always in so doing imply the reservations made by Marx. This suffices here; more is to be found in Marx's *A Contribution to the Critique of Political Economy*, 1859, and the first volume of *Capital.*[a]

But as soon as the economists applied this determination of value by labour to the commodity "labour", they fell into one contradiction after another. How is the value of "labour" determined? By the necessary labour contained in it. But how much labour is contained in the labour of a worker for a day, a week, a month, a year? The labour of a day, a week, a month, a year. If labour is the measure of all values, then indeed we can express the "value of labour" only in labour. But we know absolutely nothing about the value of an hour of labour, if we only know that it is equal to an hour of labour. This brings us not a hair's breadth nearer the goal; we keep on moving in a circle.

Classical political economy, therefore, tried another tack. It said: The value of a commodity is equal to its cost of production. But what is the cost of production of labour? In order to answer this question, the economists have to tamper a little with logic. Instead of investigating the cost of production of labour itself, which unfortunately cannot be ascertained, they proceed to investigate the cost of production of the *worker.* And this can be ascertained. It varies with time and circumstance, but for a given state of society, a given locality and a given branch of production, it too is given, at least within fairly narrow limits. We live today under the domination of capitalist production, in which a large, ever-increasing class of the population can live only if it works for the owners of the means of production – the tools, machines, raw materials and means of subsistence – in return for wages. On the basis of this mode of

[a] See *A Contribution to the Critique of Political Economy*, Chapter One, "The Commodity", as well as *Capital*, Volume I, Chapter I, "Commodities". [Ed.]

production, the cost of production of the worker consists of that quantity of the means of subsistence – or their price in money – which, on the average, is necessary to make him capable of working, keep him capable of working, and to replace him, after his departure by reason of old age, sickness or death, with a new worker – that is to say, to propagate the working class in the necessary numbers. Let us assume that the money price of these means of subsistence averages three marks a day.

Our worker, therefore, receives a wage of three marks a day from the capitalist who employs him. For this, the capitalist makes him work, say, twelve hours a day, calculating roughly as follows:

Let us assume that our worker – a machinist – has to make a part of a machine which he can complete in one day. The raw material – iron and brass in the necessary previously prepared form – costs twenty marks. The consumption of coal by the steam engine, and the wear and tear of this same engine, of the lathe and the other tools which our worker uses represent for one day, and reckoned by his share of their use, a value of one mark. The wage for one day, according to our assumption, is three marks. This makes twenty-four marks in all for our machine part. But the capitalist calculates that he will obtain, on an average, twenty-seven marks from his customers in return, or three marks more than his outlay.

Whence came the three marks pocketed by the capitalist? According to the assertion of classical political economy, commodities are, on the average, sold at their values, that is, at prices corresponding to the amount of necessary labour contained in them. The average price of our machine part – twenty-seven marks – would thus be equal to its value, that is, equal to the labour embodied in it. But of these twenty-seven marks, twenty-one marks were values already present before our machinist began work. Twenty marks were contained in the raw materials, one mark in the coal consumed during the work, or in the machines and tools which were used in the process and which were diminished in their efficiency to the value of this sum.

There remain six marks which have been added to the value of the raw material. But according to the assumption of our economists themselves, these six marks can only arise from the labour added to the raw material by our worker. His twelve hours' labour has thus created a new value of six marks. The value of his twelve hours' labour would, therefore, be equal to six marks. And thus we would at last have discovered what the "value of labour" is.

"Hold on there!" cries our machinist. "Six marks? But I have received only three marks! My capitalist swears by all that is holy that the value of my twelve hours' labour is only three marks, and if I demand six he laughs at me. How do you make that out?"

If previously we got into a vicious circle with our value of labour, we are now properly caught in an insoluble contradiction. We looked for the value of labour and we have found more than we can use. For the worker, the value of the twelve hours' labour is three marks, for the capitalist it is six marks, of which he pays three to the worker as wages and pockets three for himself. Thus labour would have not one but two values and very different values into the bargain!

The contradiction becomes still more absurd as soon as we reduce to labour time the values expressed in money. During the twelve hours' labour a new value of six marks is created. Hence, in six hours three marks – the sum which the worker receives for twelve hours' labour. For twelve hours' labour the worker receives as an equivalent value the product of six hours' labour. Either, therefore, labour has two values, of which one is double the size of the other, or twelve equals six! In both cases we get pure nonsense.

Turn and twist as we will, we cannot get out of this contradiction, as long as we speak of the purchase and sale of labour and of the value of labour. And this also happened to the economists. The last offshoot of classical political economy, the Ricardian school, was wrecked mainly by the insolubility of this contradiction. Classical political economy had got into a blind alley. The man who found the way out of this blind alley was Karl Marx.

What the economists had regarded as the cost of production of "labour" was the cost of production not of labour but of the living worker himself. And what this worker sold to the capitalist was not his labour. "As soon as his labour actually begins," says Marx, "it has already ceased to belong to him; it can therefore no longer be sold by him."[a] At the most, he might sell his future labour, that is, undertake to perform a certain amount of work in a definite time. In so doing, however, he does not sell labour (which would first have to be performed) but puts his labour power at the disposal of the capitalist for a definite time (in the case of time-work) or for the purpose of a definite output (in the case of piece-work) in return for a definite payment: he hires out, or sells, his labour power. But this labour power is intergrown with his person and is inseparable from it. Its cost of production, therefore, coincides with his cost of production; what the economists called the cost of production of labour is really the cost of production of the worker and therewith of his labour power. And so we can go back from the cost of production of labour power to the *value* of labour power and determine the amount of socially necessary labour requisite for the production of labour power of a particular quality, as Marx has done in the chapter on the buying and selling of labour power (*Capital*, Vol. I, Chapter IV, Section 3).[b]

Now what happens after the worker has sold his labour power to the capitalist, that is, placed it at the disposal of the latter in return for a wage – day wage or piece wage – agreed upon beforehand? The capitalist takes the worker into his workshop or factory, where all the things necessary for work – raw materials, auxiliary materials (coal, dyes, etc.), tools, machines – are already to be found. Here the worker begins to drudge. His daily wage may be, as above, three marks – and in this connection it does not make any difference

[a] Engels quotes from *Capital*, Volume I, Part VI, Chapter XIX, "The Transformation of the Value (and Respectively the Price) of Labour Power into Wages". [Ed.]

[b] See *Capital*, Volume I, Part II, Chapter VI, "The Buying and Selling of Labour Power". [Ed.]

whether he earns it as day wage or piece wage. Here also we again assume that in the twelve hours the worker by his labour adds a new value of six marks to the raw materials used up, which new value the capitalist realises on the sale of the finished piece of work. Out of this he pays the worker his three marks; the other three marks he keeps for himself. If, now, the worker creates a value of six marks in twelve hours, then in six hours he creates a value of three marks. He has, therefore, already repaid the capitalist the counter-value of the three marks contained in his wages when he has worked six hours for him. After six hours' labour they are both quits, neither owes the other a pfennig.

"Hold on there!" the capitalist now cries. "I have hired the worker for a whole day, for twelve hours. Six hours, however, are only half a day. So go right on working until the other six hours are up – only then shall we be quits!" And, in fact, the worker has to comply with his contract "voluntarily" entered into, according to which he has pledged himself to work twelve whole hours for a labour product which costs six hours of labour.

It is just the same with piece wages. Let us assume that our worker makes twelve items of a commodity in twelve hours. Each of these costs two marks in raw materials and depreciation and is sold at two and a half marks. Then the capitalist, on the same assumptions as before, will give the worker twenty-five pfennigs per item; that makes three marks for twelve items, to earn which the worker needs twelve hours. The capitalist receives thirty marks for the twelve items; deduct twenty-four marks for raw materials and depreciation and there remain six marks, of which he pays three marks to the worker in wages and pockets three marks. It is just as above. Here, too, the worker works six hours for himself, that is, for replacement of his wages (half an hour in each of the twelve hours) and six hours for the capitalist.

The difficulty over which the best economists came to grief, so long as they started out from the value of "labour", vanishes as soon as we start out from the value of "labour *power*" instead. In our present-day capitalist society, labour power is a commodity, a commodity like any other, and yet quite a peculiar commodity. It has, namely, the peculiar property of being a value-creating power, a source of value and, indeed, with suitable treatment, a source of more value than it itself possesses. With the present state of production, human labour power not only produces in one day a greater value than it itself possesses and costs; with every new scientific discovery, with every new technical invention, this surplus of its daily product over its daily cost increases, and therefore that portion of the labour day in which the worker works to produce the replacement of his day's wage decreases; consequently, on the other hand, that portion of the labour day in which he has to *make a present* of his labour to the capitalist without being paid for it increases.

And this is the economic constitution of the whole of our present-day society: it is the working class alone which produces all values. For value is only another expression for labour, that expression whereby in our present-day capitalist society is designated the amount of socially necessary labour contained in a particular commodity. These values produced by the workers do not, however, belong to the workers. They belong to the owners of the raw materials, machines, tools and the reserve funds which allow these owners to buy the labour power of the working class. From the whole mass of products produced by it, the working class, therefore, receives back only a part for itself. And as we have just seen, the other part, which the capitalist class keeps for itself and at most has to divide with the class of landowners, becomes larger with every new discovery and invention, while the part falling to the share of the working class (reckoned per head) either increases only very slowly and inconsiderably or not at all, and under certain circumstances may even fall.

But these discoveries and inventions which supersede each other at an ever-increasing rate, this productivity of human labour which rises day by day to an extent previously unheard of, finally give rise to a conflict in which the present-day capitalist economy must perish. On the one hand are immeasurable riches and a superfluity of products which the purchasers cannot cope with; on the other hand, the great mass of society proletarianised, turned into wage-workers, and precisely for that reason made incapable of appropriating for themselves this superfluity of products. The division of society into a small, excessively rich class and a large, propertyless class of wage-workers results in a society suffocating from its own superfluity, while the great majority of its members is scarcely, or even not at all, protected from extreme want. This state of affairs becomes daily more absurd and more unnecessary. It *must* be abolished, it *can* be abolished. A new social order is possible in which the present class differences will have disappeared and in which – perhaps after a short transitional period involving some privation, but at any rate of great value morally – through the planned utilisation and extension of the already existing enormous productive forces of all members of society, and with uniform obligation to work, the means for existence, for enjoying life, for the development and employment of all bodily and mental faculties will be available in an equal measure and in ever-increasing fulness. And that the workers are becoming more and more determined to win this new social order will be demonstrated on both sides of the ocean by May the First, tomorrow, and by Sunday, May 3.[a]

Frederick Engels
London, April 30, 1891

[a] Engels is referring to May Day festivities of 1891. In some countries, including Britain and Germany, May Day was celebrated on the first Sunday of the month, which in 1891 fell on May 3. [Ed.]

Karl Marx

WAGE LABOUR AND CAPITAL

In the second half of December 1847, Marx delivered several lectures on political economy in the German Workers' Society in Brussels and intended to prepare them for publication. A manuscript of the pamphlet prepared at the time and entitled *Wages* has survived. It is written in Joseph Weydemeyer's hand and its text is almost identical to that published later in the *Neue Rheinische Zeitung*. In 1859 Marx himself pointed out that he did not manage to publish the work on "Wage Labour" based on his lectures because of the February revolution of 1848 in France and his expulsion from Belgium.

This work first appeared as a series of leading articles in the *Neue Rheinische Zeitung* of April 5-8 and 11, 1849 under the title of *Wage Labour and Capital*. The work was not published in the newspaper in full. Issue No. 269 announced that there was to be a sequel, but this never appeared because Marx had to leave Cologne for a time and, subsequently, the *Neue Rheinische Zeitung* ceased publication due to the worsening of the political situation.

[I]

From various quarters we have been reproached with not having presented the *economic relations* which constitute the material foundation of the present class struggles and national struggles. We have designedly touched upon these relations only where they directly forced themselves to the front in political conflicts.

The point was, above all, to trace the class struggle in current history, and to prove empirically by means of the historical material already at hand and which is being newly created daily, that, with the subjugation of the working class, the class which had made February and March,[a] its opponents were simultaneously defeated – the bourgeois republicans in France and the bourgeois and peasant classes which were fighting feudal absolutism throughout the continent of Europe; that the victory of the "respectable republic" in France was at the same time the downfall of the nations that had responded to the February revolution by heroic wars of independence; finally, that Europe, with the defeat of the revolutionary workers, had relapsed into its old double slavery, the *Anglo-Russian* slavery. The June struggle in Paris, the fall of Vienna, the tragi-comedy of Berlin's November 1848, the desperate exertions of Poland, Italy and Hungary,[b] the starving of Ireland into submission – these were the concentrated expressions of the European

[a] Marx is referring to the insurrection in Paris of February 24, 1848, which led to the overthrow of King Louis-Philippe and the proclamation of the republic, and to the insurrection in Berlin of March 18-21. [Ed.]

[b] The subsequent stages of the European counter-revolution (June, 1848-August, 1849). [Ed.]

class struggle between bourgeoisie and working class, by means of which we proved that every revolutionary upheaval, however remote from the class struggle its goal may appear to be, must fail until the revolutionary working class is victorious, that every social reform remains a utopia until the proletarian revolution and the feudalistic counter-revolution measure swords in a *world war*. In our presentation, as in reality, *Belgium* and *Switzerland* were tragicomic genre-pictures akin to caricature in the great historical tableau, the one being the model state of the bourgeois monarchy, the other the model state of the bourgeois republic, both of them states which imagine themselves to be as independent of the class struggle as of the European revolution.

Now, after our readers have seen the class struggle develop in colossal political forms in 1848, the time has come to deal more closely with the economic relations themselves on which the existence of the bourgeoisie and its class rule, as well as the slavery of the workers, are founded.

We shall present in three large sections: 1) the relation of *wage labour to capital*, the slavery of the worker, the domination of the capitalist; 2) *the inevitable destruction of the middle bourgeois classes and of the so-called burgher estate*[a] *under the present system*; 3) *the commercial subjugation and exploitation of the bourgeois classes of the various European nations* by the despot of the world market – *England*.[b]

We shall try to make our presentation as simple and popular as possible and shall not presuppose even the most elementary notions of political economy. We wish to be understood by the workers. Moreover, the most remarkable ignorance and confusion of ideas prevails in Germany in regard to the simplest economic relations, from the accredited defenders of the existing state of things down to the *socialist miracle workers* and the *unrecognised political geniuses*

[a] The *Bürgerstand*, in Marx's text, i.e. the estate – in the *Ancien Régime* sense – of the burghers, comprised in the Prussian general law (*Allgemeine Landrecht für die Preussischen Staaten*, enforced in 1794) along with the *Bauernstand* (peasants) and *Adelstand* (nobles). [Ed.]

[b] Only the first of the three listed subjects is treated here; the *Neue Rheinische Zeitung* was banned in May, 1849. [Ed.]

in which fragmented Germany is even richer than in sovereign princes.

Now, therefore, for the first question: *What are wages? How are they determined?*

If workers were asked: "How much are your wages?" one would reply: "I get a mark [a] a day from my bourgeois"; another, "I get two marks", and so on. According to the different trades to which they belong, they would mention different sums of money which they receive from their respective bourgeois for a particular labour time or for the performance of a particular piece of work, for example, weaving a yard of linen or type-setting a printed sheet. In spite of the variety of their statements, they would all agree on one point: wages are the sum of money paid by the capitalist [b] a for a particular labour time or for a particular output of labour.

The capitalist, [c] it seems, therefore, *buys* their labour with money. They *sell* him their labour for money. [d] But this is merely the appearance. In reality what they sell to the capitalist for money is their labour *power.* The capitalist buys this labour power for a day, a week, a month, etc. And after he has bought it, he uses it by having the workers work for the stipulated time. For the same sum with which the bourgeois has bought their labour power, [e] for example, two marks, he could have bought two pounds of sugar or a definite amount of any other commodity. The two marks, with which he bought two pounds of sugar, are the *price* of the two pounds of sugar. The two marks, with which he bought twelve hours' use of labour power, are the

---

[a] 1 mark = 8 Prussian sgr [silver groschen] [Marx's note.] In the 1849 text the word "franc" is used everywhere instead of "mark". [Ed.]

[b] The 1849 text has "bourgeiois" here instead of "capitalist". [Ed.]

[c] The 1849 text has "bourgeiois" here instead of "capitalist" and the words "it seems" are not present. [Ed.]

[d] The following sentences, up to "... the stipulated time", were added by Engels to the 1891 edition. [Ed.]

[e] 1849: "labour". The change of "labour" into "labour power" is almost generalised and it will be from here on indicated only in connection with other amendments. [Ed.]

price of twelve hours' labour. Labour power, therefore, is a commodity, neither more nor less than sugar. The former is measured by the clock, the latter by the scales.

The workers exchange their commodity, labour power, for the commodity of the capitalist, for money, and this exchange takes place in a definite ratio. So much money for so long a use of labour power.[a] For twelve hours' weaving, two marks. And do not the two marks represent all the other commodities which I can buy for two marks? In fact, therefore, the worker has exchanged his commodity, labour power, for other commodities of all kinds and that in a definite ratio. By giving him two marks, the capitalist has given him so much meat, so much clothing, so much fuel, light, etc., in exchange for his day's labour. Accordingly, the two marks express the ratio in which labour power is exchanged for other commodities, the *exchange value* of his labour power. The exchange value of a commodity, reckoned in *money* is what is called its *price. Wages* are only a special name for the price of labour power, commonly called the *price of labour*, for the price of this peculiar commodity which has no other repository than human flesh and blood.

Let us take any worker, say, a weaver. The capitalist[b] supplies him with the loom and yarn. The weaver sets to work and the yarn is converted into linen. The capitalist takes possession of the linen and sells it, say, for twenty marks. Now are the wages of the weaver a *share* in the linen, in the twenty marks, in the product of his labour? By no means. Long before the linen is sold, perhaps long before its weaving is finished, the weaver has received his wages. The capitalist, therefore, does not pay these wages with the money which he will obtain from the linen, but with money already in reserve. Just as the loom and the yarn are not the product of the weaver to whom they are supplied by his capitalist, so likewise with the commodities which the weaver receives in exchange for his commodity, labour power. It was possible

[a] 1849: "for so much labour". [Ed.]

[b] The 1849 text has here and below "bourgeois" instead of "capitalist". [Ed.]

that the capitalist found no purchaser at all for his linen. It was possible that he did not get even the amount of the wages by its sale. It is possible that he sells it very profitably in comparison with the weaver's wages. All that has nothing to do with the weaver. The capitalist buys the labour power of the weaver with a part of his available wealth, of his capital, just as he has bought the raw material – the yarn – and the instrument of labour – the loom – with another part of his wealth. After he has made these purchases, and these purchases include the labour power necessary for the production of linen, he produces only with the raw *materials and instruments of labour belonging to him.* For the latter include now, true enough, our good weaver as well, who has as little share in the product or the price of the product as the loom has.

Wages are, therefore, not the worker's share in the commodity produced by him. Wages are the part of already existing commodities with which the capitalist buys for himself a definite amount of productive labour power.

Labour power is, therefore, a commodity which its possessor, the wage-worker, sells to capital. Why does he sell it? In order to live.

But the exercise of labour power is the worker's own life-activity, the manifestation of his own life. And this *life-activity* he sells to another person in order to secure the necessary *means of subsistence.* Thus his life-activity is for him only a means to enable him to exist. He works in order to live. He does not even reckon labour as part of his life, it is rather a sacrifice of his life. It is a commodity which he has made over to another. Hence, also, the product of his activity is not the object of his activity. What he produces for himself is not the silk that he weaves, not the gold that he draws from the mine, not the palace that he builds. What he produces for himself is *wages*, and silk, gold, palace resolve themselves for him into a definite quantity of the means of subsistence, perhaps into a cotton jacket, some copper coins and a lodging in a cellar. And the worker, who for twelve hours weaves, spins, drills, turns, builds, shovels, breaks stones, carries loads, etc. – does he consider this twelve hours' weaving, spinning, drilling, turning, building, shovelling, stone-breaking as a manifestation of his life, as life? On the contrary, life begins for him where this activity ceases, at table, in the public house, in bed. The twelve hours' labour, on the other hand, has no meaning for him as weaving, spinning, drilling, etc., but as *earnings*, which bring him to the table, to the public house, into bed. If the silkworm were to spin in order to continue its existence as a caterpillar, it would be a complete wage-worker.

Labour power was not always a *commodity*. Labour was not always wage labour, that is, *free* labour. The slave did not sell his labour power to the slave owner, any more than the ox sells its services to the peasant. The slave, together with his labour power, is sold once and for all to his owner. He is a commodity which can pass from the hand of one owner to that of another. *He is himself a commodity*, but the labour power is not *his* commodity. The *serf* sells only a part of his labour power. He does not receive a wage from the owner of the land; rather the owner of the land receives a tribute from him. The serf belongs to the land and turns over to the owner of the land the fruits thereof. The *free labourer*, on the other hand, sells himself and, indeed, sells himself piecemeal. He sells at auction eight, ten, twelve, fifteen hours of his life, day after day, to the highest bidder, to the owner of the raw materials, instruments of labour and means of subsistence, that is, to the capitalist. The worker belongs neither to an owner nor to the land, but eight, ten, twelve, fifteen hours of his daily life belong to him who buys them. The worker leaves the capitalist to whom he hires himself whenever he likes, and the capitalist discharges him whenever he thinks fit, as soon as he no longer gets any profit out of him, or not the anticipated profit. But the worker, whose sole source of livelihood is the sale of his labour power, cannot leave the *whole class of purchasers, that is, the capitalist class*, without renouncing his existence. *He belongs not to this or that capitalist, but to the capitalist class*, and it is his business to dispose of himself, that is to find a purchaser within this capitalist class.

Now, before going more closely into the relation between capital and wage labour, we shall present briefly the most general relations which come into consideration in the determination of wages.

Wages, as we have seen, are the *price* of a definite commodity, of labour power. Wages are, therefore, determined by the same laws that determine the price of every other commodity.

The question, therefore, is, *how is the price of a commodity determined*?

[II]

By what is the *price* of a commodity determined?

By competition between buyers and sellers, by the relation of inquiry to delivery, of demand to supply. Competition, by which the price of a commodity is determined, is *three-sided.*

The same commodity is offered by various sellers. With goods of the same quality, the one who sells most cheaply is certain of driving the others out of the field and securing the greatest sale for himself. Thus, the sellers mutually contend among themselves for sales, for the market. Each of them desires to sell, to sell as much as possible and, if possible, to sell alone, to the exclusion of the other sellers. Hence, one sells cheaper than another. Consequently, competition takes place *among the sellers*, which *depresses* the price of the commodities offered by them.

But *competition* also takes place *among the buyers*, which in its turn *causes* the commodities offered to *rise* in price.

Finally, *competition* occurs *between buyers and sellers*, the former desire to buy as cheaply as possible, the latter to sell as dearly as possible. The result of this competition between buyers and sellers will depend upon how the two above-mentioned sides of the competition are related, that is, whether the competition is stronger in the army of buyers or in the army of sellers. Industry leads two armies into the field against each other, each of which again carries on a battle within its own ranks, among its own troops. The army whose troops beat each other up the least gains the victory over the opposing host.

Let us suppose there are 100 bales of cotton on the market and at the same time buyers for 1,000 bales of cotton. In this case, therefore, the demand is ten times as great as the supply. Competition will be very strong among the buyers, each of whom desires to get one, and if possible all, of the hundred bales for himself. This example is no arbitrary assumption. We have experienced periods of cotton crop failure in the history of the trade, when a few capitalists in alliance have tried to buy, not one hundred bales, but all the cotton stocks of the world. Hence, in the example mentioned, one buyer will seek to drive the other from the field by offering a relatively higher price per bale of cotton. The cotton sellers, who see that the troops of the enemy army are engaged in the most violent struggle among themselves and that the sale of all their hundred bales is absolutely certain, will take good care not to fall out among themselves and depress the price of cotton at the moment when their adversaries are competing with one another to force it up. Thus, peace suddenly descends on the army of the sellers. They stand facing the buyers as *one* man, fold their arms philosophically, and there would be no bounds to their demands were it not that the offers of even the most persistent and eager buyers have very definite limits.

If, therefore, the supply of a commodity is lower than the demand for it, then only slight competition, or none at all, takes place among the sellers. In the same proportion as this competition decreases, competition increases among the buyers. The result is a more or less considerable rise in commodity prices.

It is well known that the reverse case with a reverse result occurs more frequently. Considerable surplus of supply over demand; desperate competition among the sellers; lack of buyers; disposal of goods at ridiculously low prices.

But what is the meaning of a rise, a fall in prices; what is the meaning of high price, low price? A grain of sand is high when examined through a microscope, and a tower is low when compared with a mountain. And if price is determined by the relation between demand and supply, what determines the relation between demand and supply?

Let us turn to the first bourgeois we meet. He will not reflect for an instant but, like another Alexander the Great, will cut this metaphysical knot with the multiplication table. If the production of the goods which I sell has cost me 100 marks, he will tell us, and if I get 110 marks from the sale of these goods, within the year of course – then that is sound, honest, legitimate profit. But if I get in exchange 120 or 130 marks, that is a high profit; and if I get as much as 200 marks, that would be an extraordinary, an enormous profit. What, therefore, serves the bourgeois as his measure of profit? The *cost of production* of his commodity. If he receives in exchange for this commodity an amount of other commodities which it has cost less to produce, he has lost. If he receives in exchange for his commodity an amount of other commodities the production of which has cost more, he has gained. And he calculates the fall or rise of the profit according to the degree in which the exchange value of his commodity stands below or above zero – the *cost of production.*

We have thus seen how the changing relation of demand and supply causes now a rise and now a fall of prices, now high, now low prices.

If the price of a commodity rises considerably because of inadequate supply or disproportionate increase of the demand, the price of some other commodity must necessarily have fallen proportionately, for the price of a commodity only expresses in money the ratio in which other commodities are given in exchange for it. If, for example, the price of a yard of silk material rises from five marks to six marks, the price of silver in relation to silk material has fallen and likewise the prices of all other commodities that have remained at their old prices have fallen in relation to the silk. One has to give a larger amount of them in exchange to get the same amount of silks.

What will be the consequence of the rising price of a commodity? A mass of capital will be thrown into that flourishing branch of industry and this influx of capital into the domain of the favoured industry will continue until it yields the ordinary profits or, rather, until the price of its products, through over-production, sinks below the cost of production.

Conversely, if the price of a commodity falls below its cost of production, capital will be withdrawn from the production of this commodity. Except in the case of a branch of industry which has become obsolete and must, therefore, perish, the production of such a commodity, that is, its supply, will go on decreasing owing to this flight of capital until it corresponds to the demand, and consequently its price is again on a level with its cost of production or, rather, until the supply has sunk below the demand, that is, until its price rises again above its cost of production, for the *current price of a commodity is always either above or below its cost of production.*

We see how capital continually migrates in and out, out of the domain of one industry into that of another. High prices bring too great an immigration and low prices too great an emigration.

We could show from another point of view how not only supply but also demand is determined by the cost of production. But this would take us too far away from our subject.

We have just seen how the fluctuations of supply and demand continually bring the price of a commodity back to the cost of production. *The real price of a commodity, it is true, is always above or below its cost of production; but rise and fall reciprocally balance each other,* so that within a certain period of time, taking the ebb and flow of the industry together, commodities are exchanged for one another in accordance with their cost of production, their price, therefore, being determined by their cost of production.

This determination of price by cost of production is not to be understood in the sense of the economists. The economists say that the *average price* of commodities is equal to the cost of production; that this is a *law.* The anarchical movement, in which rise is compensated by fall and fall by rise, is regarded by them as chance. With just as much right one could regard the fluctuations as the law and the determination by the cost of production as chance, as has actually been done by other economists. But it is solely these fluctuations, which, looked at more closely, bring with them the most fearful devastations and, like earthquakes, cause bourgeois society to tremble to its foundations – it is solely in the course of these fluctuations that prices are determined by the cost of production. The total movement of this disorder is its order. In the course of this industrial anarchy, in this movement in a circle, competition compensates, so to speak, for one excess by means of another.

We see, therefore, that the price of a commodity is determined by its cost of production in such manner that the periods in which the price of this commodity rises above its cost of production are compensated by the periods in which it sinks below the cost of production, and vice versa. This does not hold good, of course, for separate, particular industrial products but only for the whole branch of industry. Consequently, it also does not hold good for the individual industrialist but only for the whole class of industrialists.

The determination of price by the cost of production is equivalent to the determination of price by the labour time necessary for the manufacture of a commodity, for the cost of production consists of 1) raw materials and depreciation of instruments,[a] that is, of industrial products the production of which has cost a certain amount of labour days and which, therefore, represent a certain amount of labour time, and 2) of direct labour, the measure of which is, precisely, time.

Now, the same general laws that regulate the price of commodities in general of course also regulate *wages*, the *price of labour.*

Wages will rise and fall according to the relation of demand and supply, according to the turn taken by the competition between the buyers of labour power, the capitalists, and the sellers of labour power, the workers. The fluctuations in wages correspond in general to the fluctuations in prices of commodities. *Within these fluctuations, however, the price of labour will be determined by the cost of production, by the labour time necessary to produce this commodity – labour power.*

What, then, is the cost of production of labour power?

It is the cost required for maintaining the worker as a worker and for developing him into a worker.

---

[a] The 1849 text has "instruments of labour" here instead of "depreciation of instruments". [Ed.]

The less the period of training, therefore, that any work requires the smaller is the cost of production of the worker and the lower is the price of his labour, his wages. In those branches of industry in which hardly any period of apprenticeship is required and where the mere bodily existence of the worker suffices, the cost necessary for his production is almost confined to the commodities necessary for keeping him alive and capable of working.[a] The *price of his labour* will, therefore, be determined by the *price of the necessary means of subsistence.*

Another consideration, however, also comes in.

The manufacturer in calculating his cost of production and, accordingly, the price of the products takes into account the wear and tear of the instruments of labour. If, for example, a machine costs him 1,000 marks and wears out in ten years, he adds 100 marks annually to the price of the commodities so as to be able to replace the worn-out machine by a new one at the end of ten years. In the same way, in calculating the cost of production of simple labour power, there must be included the cost of reproduction, whereby the race of workers is enabled to multiply and to replace worn-out workers by new ones. Thus the depreciation of the worker is taken into account in the same way as the depreciation of the machine.

The cost of production of simple labour power, therefore, amounts to the *cost of existence and reproduction of the worker.* The price of this cost of existence and reproduction constitutes wages. Wages so determined are called the *wage minimum.* This wage minimum, like the determination of the price of commodities by the cost of production in general, does not hold good for the *single individual* but for the *species.* Individual workers, millions of workers, do not get enough to be able to exist and reproduce themselves; but the *wages of the whole working class* level down, within their fluctuations, to this minimum.

Now that we have arrived at an understanding of the most general laws which regulate wages like the price of any other commodity, we can go into our subject more specifically.

---

[a] The words "and capable of working" were added to the 1891 edition. [Ed.]

[III]

Capital consists of raw materials, instruments of labour and means of subsistence of all kinds, which are utilised in order to produce new raw materials, new instruments of labour and new means of subsistence. All these component parts of capital are creations of labour, products of labour, *accumulated labour*. Accumulated labour which serves as a means of new production is capital.

So say the economists.

What is a Negro slave? A man of the black race. The one explanation is as good as the other.

A Negro is a Negro. He only becomes a *slave* in certain relations. A cotton-spinning jenny is a machine for spinning cotton. It becomes *capital* only in certain relations. Torn from these relationships it is no more capital than *gold* in itself is *money* or sugar the *price* of sugar.

In production, men not only act on nature but also on one another.[a] They produce only by co-operating in a certain way and mutually exchanging their activities. In order to produce, they enter into definite connections and relations with one another and only within these social connections and relations does their action on nature,[b] does production, take place.

These social relations into which the producers enter with one another, the conditions under which they exchange their activities and participate in the whole act of production, will naturally vary according to the character of the means of production. With the invention of a new

[a] The 1849 text has "enter into relation not only with nature" instead of "not only act on nature but also on one another". [Ed.]

[b] The 1849 text has "relation with nature" instead of "action on nature". [Ed.]

instrument of warfare, firearms, the whole internal organisation of the army necessarily changed; the relationships within which individuals can constitute an army and act as an army were transformed and the relations of different armies to one another also changed.

Thus the social relations within which individuals produce, *the social relations of production, change, are transformed, with the change and development of the material means of production, the productive forces. The relations of production in their totality constitute what are called the social relations, society*, and, specifically, a society at *a definite stage of historical development*, a society with a peculiar, distinctive character. Ancient society, feudal society, bourgeois society are such totalities of production relations, each of which at the same time denotes a special stage of development in the history of mankind.

Capital, also, is a social relation of production. It is a *bourgeois production relation*, a production relation of bourgeois society. Are not the means of subsistence, the instruments of labour, the raw materials of which capital consists, produced and accumulated under given social conditions, in definite social relations? Are they not utilised for new production under given social conditions, in definite social relations? And is it not just this definite social character which turns the products serving for new production into *capital*?

Capital consists not only of means of subsistence, instruments of labour and raw materials, not only of material products; it consists just as much of *exchange values*. All the products of which it consists are *commodities*. Capital is, therefore, not only a sum of material products; it is a sum of commodities, of exchange values, of *social magnitudes*.

Capital remains the same, whether we put cotton in place of wool, rice in place of wheat or steamships in place of railways, provided only that the cotton, the rice, the steamships – the body of capital – have the same exchange value, the same price as the wool, the wheat, the railways in which it was previously incorporated. The body of capital can change continually without the capital suffering the slightest alteration.

But while all capital is a sum of commodities, that is, of exchange values, not every sum of commodities, of exchange values, is capital.

Every sum of exchange values is an exchange value. Every separate exchange value is a sum of exchange values. For instance, a house that is worth 1,000 marks is an exchange value of 1,000 marks. A piece of paper worth a pfennig[a] is a sum of exchange values of one-hundred hundredths of a pfennig. Products which are exchangeable for others are *commodities*. The particular ratio in which they are exchangeable constitutes their *exchange value* or, expressed in money, their *price*. The quantity of these products can change nothing in their quality of being *commodities* or representing an *exchange value* or having a definite *price*. Whether a tree is large or small it is a tree. Whether we exchange iron for other products in ounces or in hundredweights, does this make any difference in its character as commodity, as exchange value? It is a commodity of greater or lesser value, of higher or lower price, depending upon the quantity.

How, then, does any amount of commodities, of exchange values, become capital?

By maintaining and multiplying itself as an independent social power, that is, as the power *of a portion of society*, by means of its *exchange for direct, living labour power*. The existence of a class which possesses nothing but its capacity to labour is a necessary prerequisite of capital.

It is only the domination of accumulated, past, materialised labour over direct, living labour that turns accumulated labour into capital.

Capital does not consist in accumulated labour serving living labour as a means for new production. It consists in living labour serving accumulated labour as a means for maintaining and multiplying the exchange value of the latter.

What takes place in the exchange between capitalist and wage-worker[b]?

---

[a] In the 1849 text the word "centime" is used here and below instead of "pfennig". [Ed.]

[b] The 1849 text has "between capital and wage labour" instead of "between capitalist and wage-worker". [Ed.]

The worker receives means of subsistence in exchange for his labour power, but the capitalist receives in exchange for his means of subsistence labour, the productive activity of the worker, the creative power whereby the worker not only replaces what he consumes but gives to the accumulated labour a greater value than it previously possessed. The worker receives a part of the available means of subsistence from the capitalist. For what purpose do these means of subsistence serve him? For immediate consumption. As soon, however, as I consume the means of subsistence, they are irretrievably lost to me unless I use the time during which I am kept alive by them in order to produce new means of subsistence, in order during consumption to create by my labour new values in place of the values which perish in being consumed. But it is just this noble reproductive power that the worker surrenders to capital in exchange for means of subsistence received. He has, therefore, lost it for himself.

Let us take an example: a tenant farmer gives his day labourer five silver groschen a day. For these five silver groschen the labourer works all day on the farmer's field and thus secures him a return of ten silver groschen. The farmer not only gets the value replaced that he has to give the day labourer; he doubles it. He has therefore employed, consumed, the five silver groschen that he gave to the labourer in a fruitful, productive manner. He has bought with the five silver groschen just that labour and power of the labourer which produces agricultural products of double value and makes ten silver groschen out of five. The day labourer, on the other hand, receives in place of his productive power, the effect of which he has bargained away to the farmer, five silver groschen, which he exchanges for means of subsistence, and these he consumes with greater or less rapidity. The five silver groschen have, therefore, been consumed in a double way, *reproductively* for capital, for they have been exchanged for labour power which produced ten silver groschen, *unproductively* for the worker, for they have been exchanged for means of subsistence which have disappeared forever and the value of which he can only recover by repeating the same exchange with the farmer. *Thus capital presupposes wage labour; wage labour presupposes capital. They reciprocally condition the existence of each other; they reciprocally bring forth each other.*

Does a worker in a cotton factory produce merely cotton textiles? No, he produces capital. He produces values which serve afresh to command his labour and by means of it to create new values.

Capital can only increase by exchanging itself for labour power, by calling wage labour to life. The labour power of the wage-worker[a] can only be exchanged for capital by increasing capital, by strengthening the power whose slave it is. *Hence, increase of capital is increase of the proletariat, that is, of the working class.*

The interests of the capitalist and those of the worker are, therefore, *one and the same*, assert the bourgeois and their economists. Indeed! The worker perishes if capital does not employ him. Capital perishes if it does not exploit labour power, and in order to exploit it, it must buy it. The faster capital intended for production, productive capital, increases, the more, therefore, industry prospers, the more the bourgeoisie enriches itself and the better business is, the more workers does the capitalist need, the more dearly does the worker sell himself.

The indispensable condition for a tolerable situation of the worker is, therefore, the *fastest possible growth of productive capital.*

But what is the growth of productive capital? Growth of the power of accumulated labour over living labour. Growth of the domination of the bourgeoisie over the working class. If wage labour produces the wealth of others that rules over it, the power that is hostile to it, capital, then the means of employment, that is, the means of subsistence, flow back to it from this hostile power, on condition that it makes itself afresh into a part of capital, into the lever which hurls capital anew into an accelerated movement of growth.

---

[a] The 1849 text has "The wage labour" instead of "The labour power of the wage-worker". [Ed.]

To say that the interests of capital and those of workers are one and the same is only to say that capital and wage labour are two sides of one and the same relation. The one conditions the other, just as usurer and squanderer condition each other.

As long as the wage-worker is a wage-worker his lot depends upon capital. That is the much-vaunted community of interests between worker and capitalist.

[IV]

If capital grows, the mass of wage labour grows, the number of wage-workers grows; in a word, the domination of capital extends over a greater number of individuals. Let us assume the most favourable case: when productive capital grows, the demand for labour grows; consequently, the price of labour, wages, goes up.

A house may be large or small; as long as the surrounding houses are equally small it satisfies all social demands for a dwelling. But let a palace arise beside the little house, and it shrinks from a little house to a hut. The little house shows now that its owner has only very slight or no demands to make; and however high it may shoot up in the course of civilisation, if the neighbouring palace grows to an equal or even greater extent, the occupant of the relatively small house will feel more and more uncomfortable, dissatisfied and cramped within its four walls.

A noticeable increase in wages presupposes a rapid growth of productive capital. The rapid growth of productive capital brings about an equally rapid growth of wealth, luxury, social wants, social enjoyments. Thus, although the enjoyments of the worker have risen, the social satisfaction that they give has fallen in comparison with the increased enjoyments of the capitalist, which are inaccessible to the worker, in comparison with the state of development of society in general. Our desires and pleasures spring from society; we measure them, therefore, by society and not by the objects which serve for their satisfaction. Because they are of a social nature, they are of a relative nature.

In general, wages are determined not only by the amount of commodities for which I can exchange them. They embody various relations.

What the workers receive for their labour power is, in the first place, a definite sum of money. Are wages determined only by this money price?

In the sixteenth century, the gold and silver circulating in Europe increased as a result of the discovery of richer and more easily worked mines in America.[a] Hence, the value of gold and silver fell in relation to other commodities. The workers received the same amount of coined silver for their labour power as before. The money price of their labour remained the same, and yet their wages had fallen, for in exchange for the same quantity of silver they received a smaller amount of other commodities. This was one of the circumstances which furthered the growth of capital and the rise of the bourgeoisie in the sixteenth century.

Let us take another case. In the winter of 1847, as a result of a crop failure, the most indispensable means of subsistence, cereals, meat, butter, cheese, etc., rose considerably in price. Assume that the workers received the same sum of money for their labour power as before. Had not their wages fallen? Of course. For the same money they received less bread, meat, etc., in exchange. Their wages had fallen, not because the value of silver had diminished, but because the value of the means of subsistence had increased.

Assume, finally, that the money price of labour remains the same while all agricultural and manufactured goods have fallen in price owing to the employment of new machinery, a favourable season, etc. For the same money the workers can now buy more commodities of all kinds. Their wages, therefore, have risen, just because the money value of their wages has not changed.

Thus, the money price of labour, nominal wages, do not coincide with real wages, that is, with the sum of commodities which is actually given in exchange for the wages. If, therefore, we speak of a rise or fall of wages, we must keep in mind not only the money price of labour, the nominal wages.

But neither nominal wages, that is, the sum of money for which the worker sells himself to the capitalist, nor real

---

[a] 1849: "the discovery of America". [Ed.]

wages, that is, the sum of commodities which he can buy for this money, exhaust the relations contained in wages.

Wages are, above all, also determined by their relation to the gain, to the profit of the capitalist – comparative, relative wages.

Real wages express the price of labour in relation to the price of other commodities; relative wages, on the other hand, express the share of direct labour in the new value it has created in relation to the share which falls to accumulated labour, to capital. [a]

We said above: "Wages are not the worker's share in the commodity produced by him. Wages are the part of already existing commodities with which the capitalist buys for himself a definite amount of productive labour power." But the capitalist must replace these wages out of the price at which he sells the product produced by the worker; he must replace it in such a way that there remains to him, as a rule, a surplus over the cost of production expended by him, a profit. For the capitalist, the selling price of the commodity produced by the worker is divided into three parts: *first*, replacement of the price of the raw materials advanced by him together with replacement of the depreciation of the tools, machinery and other means of labour also advanced by him; *secondly*, the replacement of the wages advanced by him, and *thirdly*, the surplus left over, the capitalist's profit. While the first part only replaces *previously existing values*, it is clear that both the replacement of the wages and also the surplus profit of the capitalist are, on the whole, taken from the *new value created by the worker's labour* and added to the raw materials. And *in this sense*, in order to compare them with one another, we can regard both wages and profit as shares in the product of the worker. [b]

Real wages may remain the same, they may even rise, and yet relative wages may fall. Let us suppose, for example,

---

[a] 1849: "express the price of direct labour in relation to the price of accumulated labour, the relative value of wage labour and capital, the reciprocal value of the capitalist and worker". [Ed.]

[b] This paragraph (beginning with "We said above") was added by Engels to the 1891 edition. [Ed.]

that all means of subsistence have gone down in price by two-thirds while wages per day have only fallen by one-third, that is to say, for example, from three marks to two marks. Although the worker can command a greater amount of commodities with these two marks than he previously could with three marks, yet his wages have gone down in relation to the profit of the capitalist. The profit of the capitalist (for example, the manufacturer) has increased by one mark; that is, for a smaller sum of exchange values which he pays to the worker, the latter must produce a greater amount of exchange values than before. The share of capital relative to the share of labour has risen.[a] The division of social wealth between capital and labour has become still more unequal. With the same capital, the capitalist commands a greater quantity of labour. The power of the capitalist class over the working class has grown, the social position of the worker has deteriorated, has been depressed one step further below that of the capitalist.

What, then, is *the general law which determines the fall and rise of wages and profit in their reciprocal relation?*

They stand in inverse ratio to each other. Capital's share,[b] *profit, rises in the same proportion as labour's share,*[c] *wages, falls, and vice versa. Profit rises to the extent that wages fall; it falls to the extent that wages rise.*

The objection will, perhaps, be made that the capitalist can profit by a favourable exchange of his products with other capitalists, by increase of the demand for his commodity, whether as a result of the opening of new markets, or as a result of a momentarily increased demand in the old markets, etc.; that the capitalist's profit can, therefore, increase by overreaching other capitalists, independently of the rise and fall of wages, of the exchange value of labour power; or that the capitalist's profit may also rise owing to the improvement of the instruments of labour, a new application of natural forces, etc.

[a] In the 1849 text this sentence reads: "The value of capital relative to the value of labour has risen". [Ed.]

[b] 1849: "The exchange value of capital". [Ed.]

[c] 1849: "the exchange value of labour". [Ed.]

First of all, it will have to be admitted that the result remains the same, although it is brought about in reverse fashion. True, the profit has not risen because wages have fallen, but wages have fallen because the profit has risen. With the. same amount of other people's labour, the capitalist has acquired a greater amount of exchange values, without having paid more for the labour on that account; that is, therefore, labour is paid less in proportion to the net profit which it yields the capitalist.

In addition, we recall that, in spite of the fluctuations in prices of commodities, the average price of every commodity, the ratio in which it is exchanged for other commodities, is determined by its *cost of production*. Hence the overreachings within the capitalist class necessarily balance one another. The improvement of machinery, new application of natural forces in the service of production, enable a larger amount of products to be created in a given period of time with the same amount of labour and capital, but not by any means a larger amount of exchange values. If, by the use of the spinning jenny, I can turn out twice as much yarn in an hour as before its invention, say, one hundred pounds instead of fifty, then in the lon run I will receive for these hundred pounds no more commodities in exchange than formerly for the fifty pounds, because the cost of production has fallen by one-half, or because I can deliver double the product at the same cost.

Finally, in whatever proportion the capitalist class, the bourgeoisie, whether of one country or of the whole world market, shares the net profit of production within itself, the total amount of this net profit always consists only of the amount by which, on the whole, accumulated labour has been increased by direct labour. This total amount grows, therefore, in the proportion in which labour augments capital, that is, in the proportion in which profit rises in comparison with wages.

We see, therefore, that even if we remain *within the relation of capital and wage labour, the interests of capital and the interests of wage labour are diametrically opposed.*

A rapid, increase of capital is equivalent to a rapid increase of profit. Profit can only increase rapidly if the price of labour,[a] if relative wages, decrease just as rapidly. Relative wages can fall although real wages rise simultaneously with nominal wages, with the money value of labour, if they do not rise, however, in the same proportion as profit. If, for instance, in times when business is good, wages rise by five per cent, profit on the other hand by thirty per cent, then the comparative, the relative wages, have *not increased but decreased.*

Thus if the income of the worker increases with the rapid growth of capital, the social gulf that separates the worker from the capitalist increases at the same time, and the power of capital over labour, the dependence of labour on capital, likewise increases at the same time.

To say that the worker has an interest in the rapid growth of capital is only to say that the more rapidly the worker increases the wealth of others, the richer will be the crumbs that fall to him, the greater is the number of workers that can be employed and called into existence, the more can the mass of slaves dependent on capital be increased.

We have thus seen that:

Even the *most favourable situation* for the working class, the *most rapid possible growth of capital,* however much it may improve the material existence of the worker, does not remove the antagonism between his interests and the interests of the bourgeoisie, the interests of the capitalist. *Profit and wages* remain as before in *inverse proportion.*

If capital is growing rapidly, wages may rise; the profit of capital rises incomparably more rapidly. The material position of the worker has improved, but at the cost of his social position. The social gulf that divides him from the capitalist has widened.

Finally:

To say that the most favourable condition for wage labour is the most rapid possible growth of productive capital is only to say that the more rapidly the working class increases and enlarges the power that is hostile to it, the wealth that does not belong to it and that rules over it, the

---

[a] 1849: "the exchange value of labour". [Ed.]

more favourable will be the conditions under which it is allowed to labour anew at increasing bourgeois wealth, at enlarging the power of capital, content with forging for itself the golden chains by which the bourgeoisie drags it in its train.

[V]

Are *growth of productive capital and rise of wages* really so inseparably connected as the bourgeois economists maintain? We must not take their word for it. We must not even believe them when they say that the fatter capital is, the better will its slave be fed. The bourgeoisie is too enlightened, it calculates too well, to share the prejudices of the feudal lord who makes a display by the brilliance of his retinue. The conditions of existence of the bourgeoisie compel it to calculate.

We must, therefore, examine more closely:

How does the growth of productive capital affect wages?

If, on the whole, the productive capital of bourgeois society grows, a *more manifold* accumulation of labour takes place. The capitals increase in number and extent. The *numerical increase* of the capitals increases the *competition between the capitalists.* The *increasing extent* of the capitals provides the means for *bringing more powerful labour armies with more gigantic instruments of war into the industrial battlefield.*

One capitalist can drive another from the field and capture his capital only by selling more cheaply. In order to be able to sell more cheaply without ruining himself, he must produce more cheaply, that is, raise the productive power of labour as much as possible. But the productive power of labour is raised, above all, by *a greater division of labour,* by a universal introduction and continual improvement of *machinery.* The greater the labour army among whom labour is divided, the more gigantic the scale on which machinery is introduced, the more does the cost of production proportionately decrease, the more fruitful is labour. Hence, a general rivalry arises among the capitalists to increase the division of labour and machinery and to exploit them on the greatest possible scale.

If, now, by a greater division of labour, by the utilisation of new machines and their improvement, by more profitable and extensive exploitation of natural forces, one capitalist has found the means of producing with the same amount of labour or of accumulated labour a greater amount of products, of commodities, than his competitors, if he can, for example, produce a whole yard of linen in the same labour time in which his competitors weave half a yard, how will this capitalist operate?

He could continue to sell half a yard of linen at the old market price; this would, however, be no means of driving his opponents from the field and of enlarging his own sales. But in the same measure in which his production has expanded, his need to sell has also increased. The more powerful and costly means of production that he has called into life *enable* him, indeed, to sell his commodities more cheaply, they *compel* him, however, at the same time to sell more commodities, to conquer a much *larger* market for his commodities; consequently, our capitalist will sell his half yard of linen more cheaply than his competitors.

The capitalist will not, however, sell a whole yard as cheaply as his competitors sell half a yard, although the production of the whole yard does not cost him more than the half yard costs the others. Otherwise he would not gain anything extra but only get back the cost of production by the exchange. His possibly greater income would be derived from the fact of having set a larger capital into motion, but not from having made more of his capital than the others. Moreover, he attains the object he wishes to attain, if he puts the price of his goods only a small percentage lower than that of his competitors. He drives them from the field, he wrests from them at least a part of their sales, by *underselling them*. And, finally, it will be remembered that the current price always stands *above* or *below the cost of production*, according to whether the sale of the commodity occurs in a favourable or unfavourable industrial season. The percentage at which the capitalist who has employed new and more fruitful means of production sells above his real cost of production will vary, depending upon whether the market price of a yard of linen stands below or above its hitherto customary cost of production.

However, the *privileged position* of our capitalist is not of long duration; other competing capitalists introduce the same machines, the same division of labour, introduce them on the same or on a larger scale, and this introduction will become so general that the price of linen is reduced not only *below its old*, but *below its new cost of production.*

The capitalists find themselves, therefore, in the same position relative to one another as *before* the introduction of the new means of production, and if they are able to supply by these means double the product at the same price, they are *now* forced to supply the double product *below* the old price. On the basis of this new cost of production, the same game begins again. More division of labour, more machinery, enlarged scale of exploitation of division of labour and machinery. And again competition brings the same counteraction against this result.

We see how in this way the mode of production and the means of production are continually transformed, revolutionised, how *the division of labour is necessarily followed by greater division of labour, the application of machinery by still greater application of machinery, work on a large scale by work on a still larger scale.*

That is the law which again and again throws bourgeois production out of its old course and which compels capital to intensify the productive forces of labour, *because* it has intensified them – the law which gives capital no rest and continually whispers in its ear: "Go on! Go on!"

This law is none other than that which, within the fluctuations of trade periods, necessarily levels out the price of a commodity to its *cost of production.*

However powerful the means of production which a capitalist brings into the field, competition will make these means of production universal and from the moment when it has made them universal, the only result of the greater fruitfulness of his capital is that he must now supply *for the same price* ten, twenty, a hundred times as much as before. But, as he must sell perhaps a thousand times as much as before in order to outweigh the lower selling price by the greater amount of the product sold, because a more extensive sale is now necessary, not only in order to make more profit but in order to replace the cost of production – the instrument of production itself, as we have seen, becomes more and more expensive – and because this mass sale becomes a question of life and death not only for him but also for his rivals, the old struggle begins again *all the more violently the more fruitful the already discovered means of production are. The division of labour and the application of machinery, therefore, will go on anew on an incomparably greater scale.*

Whatever the power of the means of production employed may be, competition seeks to rob capital of the golden fruits of this power by bringing the price of the commodities back to the cost of production, by thus making cheaper production – the supply of ever greater amounts of products for the same total price – an imperative law to the same extent as production can be cheapened, that is, as more can be produced with the same amount of labour. Thus the capitalist would have won nothing by his own exertions but the obligation to supply more in the same labour time, in a word, *more difficult conditions for the augmentation of the value of his capital.* While, therefore, competition continually pursues him with its law of the cost of production and every weapon that he forges against his rivals recoils against himself, the capitalist continually tries to get the better of competition by incessantly introducing new machines, more expensive, it is true, but producing more cheaply, and new division of labour in place of the old, and by not waiting until competition has rendered the new ones obsolete.

If now we picture to ourselves this feverish *simultaneous* agitation on the *whole world market*, it will be comprehensible how the growth, accumulation and concentration of capital results in an uninterrupted division of labour, and in the application of new and the perfecting of old machinery precipitately and on an ever more gigantic scale.

But how do these circumstances, which are inseparable from the growth of productive capital, affect the determination of wages?

The greater *division of labour* enables *one* worker to do the work of five, ten or twenty; it therefore multiplies competition among the workers fivefold, tenfold and twentyfold. The workers do not only compete by one selling himself cheaper than another; they compete by *one* doing the work of five, ten, twenty; and the *division of labour*, introduced by capital and continually increased, compels the workers to compete among themselves in this way.

Further, as the *division of labour* increases, labour is *simplified*. The *special skill* of the worker becomes worthless. He becomes transformed into a simple, monotonous productive force that does not have to use intense bodily or intellectual faculties. His labour becomes a labour that anyone can perform. Hence, competitors crowd upon him on all sides, and besides we remind the reader that the more simple and easily learned the labour is, the lower the cost of production needed to master it, the lower do wages sink, for, like the price of every other commodity, they are determined by the cost of production.

Therefore, as labour becomes more unsatisfying, more repulsive, competition increases and wages decrease. The worker tries to keep up the amount of his wages by working more, whether by working longer hours or by producing more in one hour. Driven by want, therefore, he still further increases the evil effects of the division of labour. The result is that *the more he works the less wages he receives*, and for the simple reason that he competes to that extent with his fellow workers, hence makes them into so many competitors who offer themselves on just the same bad terms as he does himself, and that, therefore, in the last resort he *competes with himself, with himself as a member of the working class.*

Machinery brings about the same results on a much greater scale, by replacing skilled workers by unskilled, men by women, adults by children. It brings about the same results, where it is newly introduced, by throwing the hand workers onto the streets in masses, and, where it is developed, improved and replaced by more productive machinery, by discharging workers in smaller batches. We have portrayed above, in a hasty sketch, the industrial war of the capitalists among themselves; *this war has the peculiarity that its battles are won less by recruiting than by discharging the army of labour. The generals, the capitalists, compete with one another as to who can discharge most soldiers of industry.*

The economists tell us, it is true, that the workers rendered superfluous by machinery find *new* branches of employment.

They dare not assert directly that the same workers who are discharged find places in the new branches of labour. The facts cry out too loudly against this lie. They really only assert that new means of employment will open up for *other component sections of the working class*, for instance, for the portion of the young generation of workers that was ready to enter the branch of industry which has gone under. That is, of course, a great consolation for the disinherited workers. The capitalist gentlemen will never want for fresh exploitable flesh and blood, and will let the dead bury their dead.[a] This is a consolation which the bourgeois give themselves rather than one which they give the workers. If the whole class of wage-workers were to be abolished owing to machinery, how dreadful that would be for capital which, without wage labour, ceases to be capital!

Let us suppose, however, that those directly driven out of their jobs by machinery, and the entire section of the new generation that was already on the watch for this employment, *find a new occupation*. Does any one imagine that it will be as highly paid as that which has been lost? *That would contradict all the laws of economics.* We have seen how modern industry always brings with it the substitution of a more simple, subordinate occupation for the more complex and higher one.

How, then, could a mass of workers who have been thrown out of one branch of industry owing to machinery find refuge in another, unless the latter *is lower, worse paid?*

The workers who work in the manufacture of machinery itself have been cited as an exception. As soon as more machinery is demanded and used in industry, it is said, there must necessarily be an increase of machines, consequently

---

[a] See *Matthew*, 8:22. [Ed.]

of the manufacture of machines, and consequently of the employment of workers in the manufacture of machines; and the workers engaged in this branch of industry are claimed to be skilled, even educated workers.

Since the year 1840 this assertion, which even before was only half true, has lost all semblance of truth because ever more versatile machines have been employed in the manufacture of machinery, no more and no less than in the manufacture of cotton yarn, and the workers employed in the machine factories, confronted by highly elaborate machines, can only play the part of highly unelaborate machines.

But in place of the man who has been discharged owing to the machine, the factory employs maybe *three* children and *one* woman! And did not the man's wages have to suffice for the three children and a woman? Did not the minimum of wages have to suffice to maintain and to propagate the race? What, then, does this favourite bourgeois phrase prove? Nothing more than that now *four times* as many workers' lives are used up in order to gain a livelihood for *one* worker's family.

Let us sum up: *The more productive capital grows, the more the division of labour and the application of machinery expands. The more the division of labour and the application of machinery expands, the more competition among the workers expands and the more their wages contract.*

In addition, the working class gains recruits from the *higher strata of society* also; a mass of small industrialists and small rentiers are hurled down into its ranks and have nothing better to do than urgently stretch out their arms alongside those of the workers. Thus the forest of uplifted arms demanding work becomes ever thicker, while the arms themselves become ever thinner.

That the small industrialist cannot survive in a contest,[a] one of the first conditions of which is to produce on an ever greater scale, that is, precisely to be a large and not a small industrialist, is self-evident.

That the interest on capital decreases in the same measure as the mass and number of capitals increase, as capital

[a] The 1849 text has "war" instead of "contest". [Ed.]

grows ; that, therefore, the small rentier can no longer live on his interest but must throw himself into industry, and consequently, help to swell the ranks of the small industrialists and thereby of candidates for the proletariat – all this surely requires no further explanation.

Finally, as the capitalists are compelled, by the movement described above, to exploit the already existing gigantic means of production on a larger scale and to set in motion all the mainsprings of credit to this end, there is a corresponding increase in industrial earthquakes, in which the trading world can only maintain itself by sacrificing a part of wealth, of products and even of productive forces to the gods of the nether world – in a word, *crises* increase. They become more frequent and more violent, if only because, as the mass of production, and consequently the need for extended markets, grows, the world market becomes more and more contracted, fewer and fewer new markets remain available for exploitation, since every preceding crisis has subjected to world trade a market hitherto unconquered or only superficially exploited. But capital does not *live* only on labour. A lord, at once aristocratic and barbarous, it drags with it into the grave the corpses of its slaves, whole hecatombs of workers who perish in the crises. Thus we see : *if capital grows rapidly, competition among the workers grows incomparably more rapidly, that is, the means of employment, the means of subsistence, of the working class decrease proportionately so much the more, and, nevertheless, the rapid growth of capital is the most favourable condition for wage labour.*

(To be continued)

Karl Marx

WAGES, PRICE AND PROFIT

Report to the General Council of the International Workingmen's Association, June 20 and 27, 1865

Wages, Price and Profit is Marx's report read at the General Council meetings in London on June 20 and 27, 1865.
Marx's aim was to refute the theses expounded by John Weston, an English member of the General Council – an "old Owenite, now a *manufacturer* himself, a very amiable and worthy man" (Marx to Engels, November 4, 1864) – which, if they had been adopted by the IWA, would have led to denying any interest in participating in trade union struggles to improve wages. "If these two propositions [of Weston's] were to be accepted, we should be in a terrible mess, both in respect of the *Trades-Unions* here and the *infection of strikes* now prevailing on the Continent." (Marx to Engels, May 20, 1865).
This report was never published in Marx's lifetime: the General Council would have liked to publish it, but had to renounce the project due to lack of money.
The original manuscript of the report, written in English by Marx, was found among Engels' papers, after the latter's death; the first posthumous publication of this writing was the German translation published in 1898 by the theoretical journal of Social Democracy, *Die Neue Zeit*, followed in the same year by the English edition brought out by Marx's daughter, Eleanor, with the title *Value, Price and Profit*.
The title of the work, as well as the sub-titles of the first six paragraphs, are not Marx's.

[Preliminary]

Citizens,

Before entering into the subject-matter, allow me to make a few preliminary remarks.

There reigns now on the Continent a real epidemic of strikes, and a general clamour for a rise of wages. The question will turn up at our Congress. You, as the head of the International Association, ought to have settled convictions upon this paramount question. For my own part, I considered it, therefore, my duty to enter fully into the matter, even at the peril of putting your patience to a severe test.

Another preliminary remark I have to make in regard to Citizen Weston. He has not only proposed to you, but has publicly defended, in the interest of the working class, as he thinks, opinions he knows to be most unpopular with the working class. Such an exhibition of moral courage all of us must highly honour. I hope that, despite the unvarnished style of my paper, at its conclusion he will find me agreeing with what appears to me the just idea lying at the bottom of his theses, which, however, in their present form, I cannot but consider theoretically false and practically dangerous.

I shall now at once proceed to the business before us.

1) [Production and Wages]

Citizen Weston's argument rested, in fact, upon two premises: firstly, that the *amount of national production* is a *fixed thing*, a *constant* quantity or magnitude, as the mathematicians would say; secondly, that the *amount of real wages*, that is to say, of wages as measured by the quantity of the commodities they can buy, is a *fixed* amount, a *constant* magnitude.

Now, his first assertion is evidently erroneous. Year after year you will find that the value and mass of production increase, that the productive powers of the national labour increase, and that the amount of money necessary to circulate this increasing production continuously changes. What is true at the end of the year, and for different years compared with each other, is true for every average day of the year. The amount or magnitude of national production changes continuously. It is not a *constant* but a *variable* magnitude, and apart from changes in population it must be so, because of the continuous change in the *accumulation of capital* and the *productive powers of labour.* It is perfectly true that if a *rise in the general rate of wages* should take place today, that rise, whatever its ulterior effects might be, would, *by itself*, not *immediately* change the amount of production. It would, in the first instance, proceed from the existing state of things. But if *before* the rise of wages the national production was *variable*, and not *fixed*, it will continue to be variable and not fixed *after* the rise of wages.

But suppose the amount of national production to be *constant* instead of *variable.* Even then, what our friend Weston considers a logical conclusion would still remain a gratuitous assertion. If I have a given number, say eight, the *absolute* limits of this number do not prevent its parts from changing their *relative* limits. If profits were six and wages two, wages might increase to six and profits decrease to two, and still the total amount remains eight. Thus the fixed amount of production would by no means prove the fixed amount of wages. How then does our friend Weston prove this fixity? By asserting it.

But even conceding him his assertion, it would cut both ways, while he presses it only in one direction. If the amount of wages is a constant magnitude, then it can be neither increased nor diminished. If then, in enforcing a temporary rise of wages, the working men act foolishly, the capitalists, in enforcing a temporary fall of wages, would act not less foolishly. Our friend Weston does not deny that, under certain circumstances, the working men *can* enforce a rise of wages, but their amount being naturally fixed, there must follow a reaction. On the other hand, he knows also that the capitalists *can* enforce a fall of wages, and, indeed, continuously try to enforce it. According to the principle of the constancy of wages, a reaction ought to follow in this case not less than in the former. The working men, therefore, reacting against the attempt at, or the act of, lowering wages, would act rightly. They would, therefore, act rightly in enforcing a *rise* in *wages*, because every *reaction* against the lowering of wages is an *action* for raising wages. According to Citizen Weston's own principle of the *constancy of wages*, the working men ought, therefore, under certain circumstances, to combine and struggle for a rise of wages.

If he denies this conclusion, he must give up the premise from which it flows. He must not say that the amount of wages is a *constant quantity*, but that, although it cannot and must not *rise*, it can and must *fall*, whenever capital pleases to lower it. If the capitalist pleases to feed you upon potatoes instead of upon meat, and upon oats instead of upon wheat, you must accept his will as a law of political economy, and submit to it. If in one country the rate of wages is higher than in another, in the United States, for example, than in England, you must explain this difference in the rate of wages by difference between the will of the American capitalist and the will of the English capitalist, a method which would certainly very much simplify, not only the study of economic phenomena, but of all other phenomena.

But even then, we might ask, *why* the will of the American capitalist differs from the will of the English capitalist? And to answer the question you must go beyond the domain of *will*. A parson may tell me that God wills one thing in France, and another thing in England. If I summon him to explain this duality of will, he might have the brass to answer me that God wills to have one will in France and another will in England. But our friend Weston is certainly the last man to make an argument of such a complete negation of all reasoning.

The *will* of the capitalist is certainly to take as much as possible. What we have to do is not to talk about his *will*, but to inquire into his *power*, the *limits of that power*, and the *character of those limits*.

2) [Production, Wages, Profits]

The address Citizen Weston read to us might have been compressed into a nutshell.

All his reasoning amounted to this: If the working class forces the capitalist class to pay five shillings instead of four shillings in the shape of money wages, the capitalist will return in the shape of commodities four shillings' worth instead of five shillings' worth. The working class would have to pay five shillings for what, before the rise of wages, they bought with four shillings. But why is this the case? Why does the capitalist only return four shillings' worth for five shillings? Because the amount of wages is fixed. But why is it fixed at four shillings' worth of commodities? Why not at three, or two, or any other sum? If the limit of the amount of wages is settled by an economic law, independent alike of the will of the capitalist and the will of the working man, the first thing Citizen Weston had to do was to state that law and prove it. He ought then, moreover, to have proved that the amount of wages actually paid at every given moment always corresponds exactly to the necessary amount of wages, and never deviates from it. If, on the other hand, the given limit of the amount of wages is founded on the *mere will* of the capitalist, or the limits of his avarice, it is an arbitrary limit. There is nothing necessary in it. It may be changed *by* the will of the capitalist, and may, therefore, be changed *against* his will.

Citizen Weston illustrated his theory by telling you that when a bowl contains a certain quantity of soup, to be eaten by a certain number of persons, an increase in the broadness of the spoons would not produce an increase in the amount of soup. He must allow me to find this illustration rather spoony. It reminded me somewhat of the simile employed by Menenius Agrippa. When the Roman plebeians struck against the Roman patricians, the patrician Agrippa told them that the patrician belly fed the plebeian members of the body politic. Agrippa failed to show that you feed the members of one man by filling the belly of another. Citizen Weston, on his part, has forgotten that the bowl from which the workmen eat is filled with the whole produce of the national labour, and that what prevents them fetching more out of it is neither the narrowness of the bowl nor the scantiness of its contents, but only the smallness of their spoons.

By what contrivance is the capitalist enabled to return four shillings' worth for five shillings ? By raising the price of the commodity he sells. Now, does a rise and more generally a change in the prices of commodities, do the prices of commodities themselves, depend on the mere will of the capitalist ? Or are, on the contrary, certain circumstances wanted to give effect to that will ? If not, the ups and downs, the incessant fluctuations of market prices, become an insoluble riddle.

As we suppose that no change whatever has taken place either in the productive powers of labour, or in the amount of capital and labour employed, or in the value of the money wherein the values of products are estimated, but *only a change in the rate of wages*, how could that *rise of wages* affect the *prices of commodities* ? Only by affecting the actual proportion between the demand for, and the supply of, these commodities.

It is perfectly true that, considered as a whole, the working class spends, and must spend, its income upon *necessaries.* A general rise in the rate of wages would, therefore, produce a rise in the demand for, and consequently in the *market prices of, necessaries.* The capitalists who produce these necessaries would be compensated for the risen wages by the rising market prices of their commodities. But how with the other capitalists, who do *not* produce necessaries? And you must not fancy them a small body. If you consider that two-thirds of the national produce are consumed by one-fifth of the population – a member of the House of Commons stated it recently to be but one-seventh of the population – you will understand what an immense proportion of the national produce must be produced in the shape of luxuries, or be *exchanged* for luxuries, and what an immense amount of the necessaries themselves must be wasted upon flunkeys, horses, cats, and so forth, a waste we know from experience to become always much limited with the rising prices of necessaries.

Well, what would be the position of those capitalists who do *not* produce necessaries? For the *fall in the rate of profit,* consequent upon the general rise of wages, they could not compensate themselves by a *rise in the price of their commodities,* because the demand for those commodities would not have increased. Their income would have decreased, and from this decreased income they would have to pay more for the same amount of higher-priced necessaries. But this would not be all. As their income had diminished they would have less to spend upon luxuries, and therefore their mutual demand for their respective commodities would diminish. Consequent upon this diminished demand the prices of their commodities would fall. In these branches of industry, therefore, *the rate of profit would fall,* not only in simple proportion to the general rise in the rate of wages, but in the compound ratio of the general rise of wages, the rise in the prices of necessaries, and the fall in the prices of luxuries.

What would be the consequence of *this difference in the rates of profit* for capitals employed in the different branches of industry? Why, the consequence that generally obtains whenever, from whatever reason, *the average rate of profit* comes to differ in the different spheres of production. Capital and labour would be transferred from the less remunerative to the more remunerative branches; and this process of transfer would go on until the supply in the one department of industry would have risen proportionately to the increased demand, and would have sunk in the other departments according to the decreased demand. *This change effected*, the *general rate of profit* would again be *equalised* in the different branches. As the whole derangement originally arose from a mere change in the proportion of the demand for, and the supply of, different commodities, the cause ceasing, the effect would cease, and *prices* would return to their former level and equilibrium. Instead of being limited to some branches of industry, the *fall in the rate of profit* consequent upon the rise of wages would have become *general.* According to our supposition, there would have taken place no change in the productive powers of labour, nor in the aggregate amount of production, but *that given amount of production would have changed its form.* A greater part of the produce would exist in the shape of necessaries, a lesser part in the shape of luxuries, or what comes to the same, a lesser part would be exchanged for foreign luxuries, and be consumed in its original form, or, what again comes to the same, a greater part of the native produce would be exchanged for foreign necessaries instead of for luxuries. The general rise in the rate of wages would, therefore, after a temporary disturbance of market prices, only result in a general fall of the rate of profit without any permanent change in the prices of commodities.

If I am told that in the previous argument I assume the whole surplus wages to be spent upon necessaries, I answer that I have made the supposition most advantageous to the opinion of Citizen Weston. If the surplus wages were spent upon articles formerly not entering into the consumption of the working men, the real increase of their purchasing power would need no proof. Being, however, only derived from an advance of wages, that increase of their purchasing power must exactly correspond to the decrease of the purchasing power of the capitalists. The *aggregate demand* for commodities would, therefore, not *increase*, but the constituent parts of that demand would *change*. The increasing demand on the one side would be counterbalanced by the decreasing demand on the other side. Thus the aggregate demand remaining stationary, no change whatever could take place in the market prices of commodities.

You arrive, therefore, at this dilemma: Either the surplus wages are equally spent upon all articles of consumption – then the expansion of demand on the part of the working class must be compensated by the contraction of demand on the part of the capitalist class – or the surplus wages are only spent upon some articles whose market prices will temporarily rise. Then the consequent rise in the rate of profit in some, and the consequent fall in the rate of profit in other branches of industry will produce a change in the distribution of capital and labour, going on until the supply is brought up to the increased demand in the one department of industry, and brought down to the diminished demand in the other departments of industry. On the one supposition there will occur no change in the prices of commodities. On the other supposition, after some fluctuations of market prices, the exchangeable values of commodities will subside to the former level. On both suppositions the general rise in the rate of wages will ultimately result in nothing else but a general fall in the rate of profit.

To stir up your powers of imagination Citizen Weston requested you to think of the difficulties which a general rise of English agricultural wages from nine shillings to eighteen shillings would produce. Think, he exclaimed, of the immense rise in the demand for necessaries, and the consequent fearful rise in their prices! Now, all of you know that the average wages of the American agricultural labourer amount to more than double that of the English agricultural labourer, although the prices of agricultural produce are lower in the United States than in the United Kingdom, although the general relations of capital and labour obtain in the United States the same as in England,

and although the annual amount of production is much smaller in the United States than in England. Why, then, does our friend ring this alarum bell? Simply to shift the real question before us. A sudden rise of wages from nine shillings to eighteen shillings would be a sudden rise to the amount of 100 per cent. Now, we are not at all discussing the question whether the general rate of wages in England could be suddenly increased by 100 per cent. We have nothing at all to do with the *magnitude* of the rise, which in every practical instance must depend on, and be suited to, given circumstances. We have only to inquire how a general rise in the rate of wages, even if restricted to one per cent., will act.

Dismissing friend Weston's fancy rise of 100 per cent., I propose calling your attention to the real rise of wages that took place in Great Britain from 1849 to 1859.

You are all aware of the Ten Hours' Bill, or rather Ten-and-a-Half Hours' Bill, introduced since 1848. This was one of the greatest economic changes we have witnessed. It was a sudden and compulsory rise of wages, not in some local trades, but in the leading industrial branches by which England sways the markets of the world. It was a rise of wages under circumstances singularly unpropitious. Dr. Ure, Professor Senior, and all the other official economical mouthpieces of the middle class, *proved*, and I must say upon much stronger grounds than those of our friend Weston, that it would sound the death-knell of English industry. They proved that it not only amounted to a simple rise of wages, but to a rise of wages initiated by, and based upon, a diminution of the quantity of labour employed. They asserted that the twelfth hour you wanted to take from the capitalist was exactly the only hour from which he derived his profit. They threatened a decrease of accumulation, rise of prices, loss of markets, stinting of production, consequent reaction upon wages, ultimate ruin. In fact, they declared Maximilien Robespierre's Maximum Laws to be a small affair compared to it; and they were right in a certain sense. Well, what was the result? A rise in the money wages of the factory operatives, despite the curtailing of the working day, a great increase in the number of factory hands employed, a continuous fall in the prices of their products, a marvellous development in the productive powers of their labour, an unheard-of progressive expansion of the markets for their commodities. In Manchester, at the meeting, in 1861, of the Society for the Advancement of Science, I myself heard Mr. *Newman*[a] confess that he, Dr. Ure, Senior, and all other official propounders of economic science had been wrong, while the instinct of the people had been right. I mention Mr. W. Newman, not Professor Francis Newman, because he occupies an eminent position in economic science, as the contributor to, and editor of, Mr. Thomas Tooke's *History of Prices*, that magnificent work which traces the history of prices from 1793 to 1856. If our friend Weston's fixed idea of a fixed amount of wages, a fixed amount of production, a fixed degree of the productive power of labour, a fixed and permanent will of the capitalists, and all his other fixedness and finality were correct, Professor Senior's woeful forebodings would have been right, and Robert Owen, who already in 1815 proclaimed a general limitation of the working day the first preparatory step to the emancipation of the working class and actually in the teeth of the general prejudice inaugurated it on his own hook in his cotton factory at New Lanark, would have been wrong.

In the very same period during which the introduction of the Ten Hours' Bill, and the rise of wages consequent upon it, occurred, there took place in Great Britain, for reasons which it would be out of place to enumerate here, *a general rise in agricultural wages.*

Although it is not required for my immediate purpose, in order not to mislead you, I shall make some preliminary remarks.

If a man got two shillings weekly wages, and if his wages rose to four shillings, the *rate of wages* would have risen by 100 per cent. This would seem a very magnificent thing if expressed as a rise in the *rate of wages*, although the

---

[a] Here and below inaccuracy in the manuscript. Should be the English statistician W. Newmarch. [Ed.]

actual amount of wages, four shillings weekly, would still remain a wretchedly small, a starvation pittance. You must not, therefore, allow yourselves to be carried away by the high-sounding per cents in the *rate* of wages. You must always ask, What was the *original* amount?

Moreover, you will understand, that if there were ten men receiving each 2s. per week, five men receiving each 5s. and five men receiving 11s. weekly, the twenty men together would receive 100s., or £5, weekly.[a] If then a rise, say by 20 per cent., upon the *aggregate* sum of their weekly wages took place, there would be an advance from £5 to £6. Taking the average, we might say that the *general rate of wages* had risen by 20 per cent., although, in fact, the wages of the ten men had remained stationary, the wages of the one lot of five men had risen from 5s. to 6s. only, and the wages of the other lot of five men from 55s. to 70s. One-half of the men would not have improved at all their position, one-quarter would have improved it in an imperceptible degree, and only one-quarter would have bettered it really. Still, reckoning by the *average*, the total amount of the wages of those twenty men would have increased by 20 per cent., and as far as the aggregate capital that employs them, and the prices of the commodities they produce, are concerned, it would be exactly the same as if all of them had equally shared in the average rise of wages. In the case of agricultural labour, the standard wages being very different in the different counties of England and Scotland, the rise affected them very unequally.

Lastly, during the period when that rise of wages took place counteracting influences were at work, such as the new taxes consequent upon the Russian war,[b] the extensive demolition of the dwelling-houses of the agricultural labourers, and so forth.

Having premised so much, I proceed to state that from 1849 to 1859 there took place a *rise of about 40 per cent.* in the average rate of the agricultural wages of Great Britain.

---

[a] One sterling pound (£) = 20 shillings (s.) of 12 pence (d.) each = 240 pence. [Ed.]

[b] The Crimean War of 1853-56. [Ed.]

I could give you ample details in proof of my assertion, but for the present purpose think it sufficient to refer you to the conscientious and critical paper read in 1859 by the late Mr. *John C. Morton* at the London Society of Arts, on *The Forces Used in Agriculture.* Mr. Morton gives the returns, from bills and other authentic documents, which he had collected from about one hundred farmers, residing in twelve Scotch and thirty-five English counties.

According to our friend Weston's opinion, and taken together with the simultaneous rise in the wages of the factory operatives, there ought to have occurred a tremendous rise in the prices of agricultural produce during the period 1849 to 1859. But what is the fact? Despite the Russian war, and the consecutive unfavourable harvests from 1854 to 1856, the average price of wheat, which is the leading agricultural produce of England, fell from about £3 per quarter for the years 1838 to 1848 to about £2 10s. per quarter for the years 1849 to 1859. This constitutes a fall in the price of wheat of more than 16 per cent. simultaneously with an average rise of agricultural wages of 40 per cent. During the same period, if we compare its end with its beginning, 1859 with 1849, there was a decrease of official pauperism from 934,419 to 860,470, the difference being 73,949; a very small decrease, I grant, and which in the following years was again lost, but still a decrease.

It might be said that, consequent upon the abolition of the Corn Laws,[a] the import of foreign corn was more than doubled during the period from 1849 to 1859, as compared with the period from 1838 to 1848. And what of that? From Citizen Weston's standpoint one would have expected that this sudden, immense, and continuously increasing demand upon foreign markets must have sent up the prices of agricultural produce there to a frightful height, the effect of

[a] Protectionist laws passed in 1815 which prevented imports of cereals into Britain below a certain price. They protected the landlords from international competition, but, by provoking tension over wages, ran counter to the interests of industry. The initiative of the Anti-Corn Law League which succeeded, in 1846, in obtaining the abolition of these laws, was launched by the Manchester industrialists in 1839. [Ed.]

increased demand remaining the same, whether it comes from without or from within. What was the fact? Apart from some years of failing harvests, during all the period the ruinous fall in the price of corn formed a standing theme of declamation in France; the Americans were again and again compelled to burn their surplus of produce; and Russia, if we are to believe Mr. Urquhart, prompted the Civil War in the United States because her agricultural exports were crippled by the Yankee competition in the markets of Europe.

Reduced to its abstract form, Citizen Weston's argument would come to this: Every rise in demand occurs always on the basis of a given amount of production. It can, therefore, *never increase the supply of the articles demanded*, but can *only enhance their money prices*. Now the most common observation shows that an increased demand will, in some instances, leave the market prices of commodities altogether unchanged, and will, in other instances, cause a temporary rise of market prices followed by an increased supply, followed by a reduction of the prices to their original level, and in many cases *below* their original level. Whether the rise of demand springs from surplus wages, or from any other cause does not at all change the conditions of the problem. From Citizen Weston's standpoint the general phenomenon was as difficult to explain as the phenomenon occurring under the exceptional circumstances of a rise of wages. His argument had, therefore, no peculiar bearing whatever upon the subject we treat. It only expressed his perplexity at accounting for the laws by which an increase of demand produces an increase of supply, instead of an ultimate rise of market prices.

3) [Wages and Currency]

On the second day of the debates our friend Weston clothed his old assertions in new forms. He said: Consequent upon a general rise in money wages, more currency will be wanted to pay the same wages. The currency being *fixed*, how can you pay with this fixed currency increased money wages? First the difficulty arose from the fixed amount of commodities accruing to the working man, despite his increase of money wages; now it arises from the increased money wages, despite the fixed amount of commodities. Of course, if you reject his original dogma, his secondary grievance will disappear.

However, I shall show that this currency question has nothing at all to do with the subject before us.

In your country the mechanism of payments is much more perfected than in any other country of Europe. Thanks to the extent and concentration of the banking system, much less currency is wanted to circulate the same amount of values, and to transact the same or a greater amount of business. For example, as far as wages are concerned, the English factory operative pays his wages weekly to the shopkeeper, who sends them weekly to the banker, who returns them weekly to the manufacturer, who again pays them away to his working men, and so forth. By this contrivance the yearly wages of an operative, say of £52, may be paid by one single sovereign turning round every week in the same circle. Even in England the mechanism is less perfect than in Scotland, and is not everywhere equally perfect; and therefore we find, for example, that in some agricultural districts, as compared with the mere factory districts, much more currency is wanted to circulate a much smaller amount of values.

If you cross the Channel, you will find that the *money wages* are much lower than in England, but that they are circulated in Germany, Italy, Switzerland, and France by a *much larger amount of currency*. The same sovereign will not be so quickly intercepted by the banker or returned to the industrial capitalist; and, therefore, instead of one sovereign circulating £52 yearly, you want, perhaps, three sovereigns to circulate yearly wages to the amount of £25. Thus, by comparing continental countries with England, you will see at once that low money wages may require a much larger currency for their circulation than high money wages, and that this is, in fact, a merely technical point, quite foreign to our subject.

According to the best calculations I know, the yearly income of the working class of this country may be estimated at £250,000,000. This immense sum is circulated by about £3,000,000. Suppose a rise of wages of 50 per cent. to take place. Then, instead of £3,000,000 of currency, £4,500,000 would be wanted. As a very considerable part of the working man's daily expenses is laid out in silver and copper, that is to say, in mere tokens, whose relative value to gold is arbitrarily fixed by law, like that of inconvertible money paper, a rise of money wages by 50 per cent. would, in the extreme case, require an additional circulation of sovereigns, say to the amount of one million. One million, now dormant, in the shape of bullion or coin, in the cellars of the Bank of England, or of private bankers, would circulate. But even the trifling expense resulting from the additional minting or the additional wear and tear of that million might be spared, and would actually be spared, if any friction should arise from the want of the additional currency. All of you know that the currency of this country is divided into two great departments. One sort, supplied by bank-notes of different descriptions, is used in the transactions between dealers and dealers, and the larger payments from consumers to dealers, while another sort of currency, metallic coin, circulates in the retail trade. Although distinct, these two sorts of currency intermix with each other. Thus gold coin, to a very great extent, circulates even in larger payments for all the odd sums under £5. If tomorrow £4 notes, or £3 notes, or £2 notes were issued, the gold filling these channels of circulation would at once be driven out of them, and flow into those channels where it would be needed from the increase of money wages. Thus the additional million required by an advance of wages by 50 per cent. would be supplied without the addition of one single sovereign. The same effect might be produced, without one additional bank-note, by an additional bill circulation, as was the case in Lancashire for a very considerable time.

If a general rise in the rate of wages, for example, of 100 per cent., as Citizen Weston supposed it to take place in agricultural wages, would produce a great rise in the prices of necessaries, and, according to his views, require an additional amount of currency not to be procured, *a general fall in wages* must produce the same effect, on the same scale, in an opposite direction. Well! All of you know that the years 1858 to 1860 were the most prosperous years for the cotton industry, and that peculiarly the year 1860 stands in that respect unrivalled in the annals of commerce, while at the same time all other branches of industry were most flourishing. The wages of the cotton operatives and of all the other working men connected with their trade stood, in 1860, higher than ever before. The American crisis came, and those aggregate wages were suddenly reduced to about one-fourth of their former amount. This would have been in the opposite direction a rise of 300 per cent. If wages rise from five to twenty, we say that they rise by 300 per cent.; if they fall from twenty to five, we say that they fall by 75 per cent., but the amount of rise in the one and the amount of fall in the other case would be the same, namely, fifteen shillings. This, then, was a sudden change in the rate of wages unprecedented, and at the same time extending over a number of operatives which, if we count all the operatives not only directly engaged in but indirectly dependent upon the cotton trade, was larger by one-half than the number of agricultural labourers. Did the price of wheat fall? It rose from the annual average of 47s. 8d. per quarter during the three years of 1858 to 1860 to the annual average of 55s. 10d. per quarter during the three years 1861-63. As to the currency, there were coined in the mint in 1861 £8,673,232, against £3,378,102 in 1860. That is to say, there were coined £5,295,130 more in 1861 than in 1860. It is true the bank-note circulation was in 1861 less by £1,319,000 than in 1860. Take this off. There remains still an overplus of currency for the year 1861, as compared with the prosperity year, 1860, to the amount of £3,976,130, or about £4,000,000; but the bullion reserve in the Bank of England had simultaneously decreased, not quite to the same, but in an approximating proportion.

Compare the year 1862 with 1842. Apart from the immense increase in the value and amount of commodities circulated, in 1862 the capital paid in regular transactions for shares, loans, etc., for the railways in England and Wales amounted alone to £320,000,000, a sum that would have appeared fabulous in 1842. Still, the aggregate amounts in currency in 1862 and 1842 were pretty nearly equal, and generally you will find a tendency to a progressive diminution of currency in the face of an enormously increasing value, not only of commodities, but of monetary transactions generally. From our friend Weston's standpoint this is an unsolvable riddle.

Looking somewhat deeper into this matter, he would have found that, quite apart from wages, and supposing them to be fixed, the value and mass of the commodities to be circulated, and generally the amount of monetary transactions to be settled, vary daily; that the amount of bank-notes issued varies daily; that the amount of payments realised without the intervention of any money, by the instrumentality of bills, checks, bookcredits, clearing houses, varies daily; that, as far as actual metallic currency is required, the proportion between the coin in circulation and the coin and bullion in reserve or sleeping in the cellars of banks varies daily; that the amount of bullion absorbed by the national circulation and the amount being sent abroad for international circulation vary daily. He would have found that his dogma of a fixed currency is a monstrous error, incompatible with the everyday movement. He would have inquired into the laws which enable a currency to adapt itself to circumstances so continually changing, instead of turning his misconception of the laws of currency into an argument against a rise of wages.

4) [Supply and Demand]

Our friend Weston accepts the Latin proverb that *repetitio est mater studiorum*, that is to say, that repetition is the mother of study, and consequently he repeated his original dogma again under the new form that the contraction of currency, resulting from an enhancement of wages, would produce a diminution of capital, and so forth. Having already dealt with his currency crotchet, I consider it quite useless to enter upon the imaginary consequences he fancies to flow from his imaginary currency mishap. I shall proceed to at once reduce his *one and the same dogma*, repeated in so many different shapes, *to its simplest theoretical form.*

The uncritical way in which he has treated his subject will become evident from one single remark. He pleads against a rise of wages or against high wages as the result of such a rise. Now, I ask him, What are high wages and what are low wages? Why constitute, for example, five shillings weekly low, and twenty shillings weekly high, wages? If five is low as compared with twenty, twenty is still lower as compared with two hundred. If a man was to lecture on the thermometer, and commenced by declaiming on high and low degrees, he would impart no knowledge whatever. He must first tell me how the freezing-point is found out, and how the boiling-point, and how these standard points are settled by natural laws, not by the fancy of the sellers or makers of thermometers. Now, in regard to wages and profits, Citizen Weston has not only failed to deduce such standard points from economical laws, but he has not even felt the necessity to look after them. He satisfied himself with the acceptance of the popular slang terms of low and high as something having a fixed meaning, although it is self-evident that wages can only be said to be high or low as compared with a standard by which to measure their magnitudes.

He will be unable to tell me why a certain amount of money is given for a certain amount of labour. If he should answer me, "This was settled by the law of supply and demand," I should ask him, in the first instance, by what law supply and demand are themselves regulated. And such an answer would at once put him out of court. The relations between the supply and demand of labour undergo perpetual change, and with them the market prices of labour. If the demand overshoots the supply wages rise; if the supply overshoots the demand wages sink, although it might in such circumstances be necessary to test the real state of demand and supply by a strike, for example, or any other method. But if you accept supply and demand as the law regulating wages, it would be as childish as useless to declaim against a rise of wages, because, according to the supreme law you appeal to, a periodical rise of wages is quite as necessary and legitimate as a periodical fall of wages. If you do *not* accept supply and demand as the law regulating wages, I again repeat the question, why a certain amount of money is given for a certain amount of labour?

But to consider matters more broadly: You would be altogether mistaken in fancying that the value of labour or any other commodity whatever is ultimately fixed by supply and demand. Supply and demand regulate nothing but the temporary *fluctuations* of market prices. They will explain to you why the market price of a commodity rises above or sinks below its *value*, but they can never account for that value itself. Suppose supply and demand to equilibrate, or, as the economists call it, to cover each other. Why, the very moment these opposite forces become equal they paralyse each other, and cease to work in the one or the other direction. At the moment when supply and demand equilibrate each other, and therefore cease to act, the market price of a commodity coincides with its *real value*, with the standard price round which its market prices oscillate. In inquiring into the nature of that *value*, we have, therefore, nothing at all to do with the temporary effects on market prices of supply and demand. The same holds true of wages and of the prices of all other commodities.

5) [Wages and Prices]

Reduced to their simplest theoretical expression, all our friend's arguments resolve themselves into this one single dogma: "*The prices of commodities are determined or regulated by wages.*"

I might appeal to practical observation to bear witness against this antiquated and exploded fallacy. I might tell you that the English factory operatives, miners, shipbuilders, and so forth, whose labour is relatively high-priced, undersell, by the cheapness of their produce, all other nations; while the English agricultural labourer, for example, whose labour is relatively low-priced, is undersold by almost every other nation, because of the dearness of his produce. By comparing article with article in the same country, and the commodities of different countries, I might show, apart from some exceptions more apparent than real, that on an average the high-priced labour produces the low-priced, and the low-priced labour produces the high-priced commodities. This, of course, would not prove that the high price of labour in the one, and its low price in the other instance, are the respective causes of those diametrically opposed effects, but at all events it would prove that the prices of commodities are not ruled by the prices of labour. However, it is quite superfluous for us to employ this empirical method.

It might, perhaps, be denied that Citizen Weston has put forward the dogma: "*The prices of commodities are determined or regulated by wages.*" In point of fact, he has never formulated it. He said, on the contrary, that profit and rent form also constituent parts of the prices of commodities, because it is out of prices of commodities that not only the working man's wages, but also the capitalist's profits and the landlord's rents must be paid. But how, in his idea, are prices formed? First by wages. Then an additional percentage is joined to the price on behalf of the capitalist, and another additional percentage on behalf of the landlord. Suppose the wages of the labour employed in the production of a commodity to be ten. If the rate of profit was 100 per cent. to the wages advanced, the capitalist would add ten, and if the rate of rent was also 100 per cent. upon the wages, there would be added ten more, and the aggregate price of the commodity would amount to thirty. But such a determination of prices would be simply their determination by wages. If wages in the above case rose to twenty, the price of the commodity would rise to sixty, and so forth. Consequently all the superannuated writers on political economy, who propounded the dogma that wages regulate prices, have tried to prove it by treating profit and rent *as mere additional percentages upon wages.* None of them were, of course, able to reduce the limits of those percentages to any economic law. They seem, on the contrary, to think profits settled by tradition, custom, the will of the capitalist, or by some other equally arbitrary and inexplicable method. If they assert that they are settled by the competition between the capitalists, they say nothing. That competition is sure to equalise the different rates of profit in different trades, or reduce them to one average level, but it can never determine the level itself, or the general rate of profit.

What do we mean by saying that the prices of the commodities are determined by wages? Wages being but a name for the price of labour, we mean that the prices of commodities are regulated by the price of labour. As "*price*" is exchangeable value – and in speaking of value I speak always of exchangeable value – is exchangeable *value expressed in money,* the proposition comes to this, that "the *value of commodities is determined by the value of labour*", or that "the *value of labour is the general measure of value*".

But how, then, is the "*value of labour*" itself determined? Here we come to a standstill. Of course, to a standstill if we try reasoning logically. Yet the propounders of that doctrine make short work of logical scruples. Take our friend Weston, for example. First he told us that wages regulate the price of commodities and that consequently when wages rise prices must rise. Then he turned round to show us that a rise of wages will be no good because the prices of commodities had risen, and because wages were indeed measured by the prices of the commodities upon which they are spent. Thus we begin by saying that the value of labour determines the value of commodities, and we wind up by saying that the value of commodities determines the value of labour. Thus we move to and fro in the most vicious circle, and arrive at no conclusion at all.

On the whole it is evident that by making the value of one commodity, say labour, corn, or any other commodity, the general measure and regulator of value, we only shift the difficulty, since we determine one value by another, which on its side wants to be determined.

The dogma that "wages determine the prices of commodities", expressed in its most abstract terms, comes to this, that "value is determined by value", and this tautology means that, in fact, we know nothing at all about value. Accepting this premise, all reasoning about the general laws of political economy turns into mere twaddle. It was, therefore, the great merit of Ricardo that in his work *On the Principles of Political Economy*, published in 1817, he fundamentally destroyed the old, popular, and worn-out fallacy that "wages determine prices", a fallacy which Adam Smith and his French predecessors had spurned in the really scientific parts of their researches, but which they reproduced in their more exoterical and vulgarising chapters.

6) [Value and Labour]

Citizens, I have now arrived at a point where I must enter upon the real development of the question. I cannot promise to do this in a very satisfactory way, because to do so I should be obliged to go over the whole field of political economy. I can, as the French would say, but *effleurer la question*, touch upon the main points.

The first question we have to put is : What is the *value* of a commodity ? How is it determined ?

At first sight it would seem that the value of a commodity is a thing quite *relative*, and not to be settled without considering one commodity in its relations to all other commodities. In fact, in speaking of the value, the value in exchange of a commodity, we mean the proportional quantities in which it exchanges with all other commodities. But then arises the question : How are the proportions in which commodities exchange with each other regulated?

We know from experience that these proportions vary infinitely. Taking one single commodity, wheat, for instance, we shall find that a quarter of wheat exchanges in almost countless variations of proportion with different commodities. Yet, *its value remaining always the same*, whether expressed in silk, gold, or any other commodity, it must be something distinct from, and independent of, these *different rates of exchange* with different articles. It must be possible to express, in a very different form, these various equations with various commodities.

Besides, if I say a quarter of wheat exchanges with iron in a certain proportion, or the value of a quarter of wheat is expressed in a certain amount of iron, I say that the value of wheat and its equivalent in iron are equal *to some third thing*, which is neither wheat nor iron, because I suppose them to express the same magnitude in two different shapes. Either of them, the wheat or the iron, must, therefore, independently of the other, be reducible to this third thing which is their common measure.

To elucidate this point I shall recur to a very simple geometrical illustration. In comparing the areas of triangles of all possible forms and magnitudes, or comparing triangles with rectangles, or any other rectilinear figure, how do we proceed? We reduce the area of any triangle whatever to an expression quite different from its visible form. Having found from the nature of the triangle that its area is equal to half the product of its base by its height, we can then compare the different values of all sorts of triangles, and of all rectilinear figures whatever, because all of them may be dissolved into a certain number of triangles.

The same mode of procedure must obtain with the values of commodities. We must be able to reduce all of them to an expression common to all, distinguishing them only by the proportions in which they contain that identical measure.

As the *exchangeable values* of commodities are only *social functions* of those things, and have nothing at all to do with their *natural* qualities, we must first ask, What is the common *social substance* of all commodities? It is *Labour*. To produce a commodity a certain amount of labour must be bestowed upon it, or worked up in it. And I say not only *Labour*, but *social Labour*. A man who produces an article for his own immediate use, to consume it himself, creates a *product*, but not a *commodity*. As a self-sustaining producer he has nothing to do with society. But to produce a commodity, a man must not only produce an article satisfying some *social* want, but his labour itself must form part and parcel of the total sum of labour expended by society. It must be subordinate to the *Division of Labour within Society*. It is nothing without the other divisions of labour, and on its part is required to *integrate* them.

If we consider *commodities as values*, we consider them exclusively under the single aspect of *realised, fixed*, or, if you like, *crystallised social labour*. In this respect they can *differ* only by representing greater or smaller quantities of labour, as, for example, a greater amount of labour may be worked up in a silken handkerchief than in a brick. But how does one measure *quantities of labour*? By the *time the labour lasts*, in measuring the labour by the hour, the day, etc. Of course, to apply this measure, all sorts of labour are reduced to average or simple labour as their unit.

We arrive, therefore, at this conclusion. A commodity has a *value*, because it is a *crystallisation of social labour*. The greatness of its value, or its relative value, depends upon the greater or less amount of that social substance contained in it; that is to say, on the relative mass of labour necessary for its production. The *relative values of commodities* are, therefore, determined by the *respective quantities* or *amounts of labour, worked up, realised, fixed in them*. The *correlative* quantities of commodities which can be produced in the *same time of labour* are *equal*. Or the value of one commodity is to the value of another commodity as the quantity of labour fixed in the one is to the quantity of labour fixed in the other.

I suspect that many of you will ask, Does then, indeed, there exist such a vast, or any difference whatever, between determining the values of commodities by *wages*, and determining them by the *relative quantities of labour* necessary for their production? You must, however, be aware that the *reward* for labour, and *quantity* of labour, are quite disparate things. Suppose, for example, *equal quantities of labour* to be fixed in one quarter of wheat and one ounce of gold. I resort to the example because it was used by *Benjamin Franklin* in his first Essay published in 1729, and entitled, *A Modest Inquiry into the Nature and Necessity of a Paper Currency*, where he, one of the first, hit upon the true nature of value. Well. We suppose, then, that one quarter of wheat and one ounce of gold are *equal values* or *equivalents*, because they are *crystallisations of equal amounts of average labour*, of so many days' or so many weeks' labour respectively fixed in them. In thus determining the relative values of gold and corn, do we refer in any way whatever to the *wages* of the agricultural labourer and the miner? Not a bit. We leave it quite *indeterminate how* their day's or week's labour was paid, or even whether wages labour was employed at all. If it was, wages may have been very unequal. The labourer whose labour is realised in the quarter of wheat may receive two bushels [a] only, and the labourer employed in mining may receive one-half of the ounce of gold. Or, supposing their wages to be equal, they may deviate in all possible proportions from the values of the commodities produced by them. They may amount to one-half, one-third, one-fourth, one-fifth, or any other proportional part of the one quarter of corn or the one ounce of gold. Their *wages* can, of course, not *exceed*, not be *more* than the values of the commodities they produced, but they can be *less* in every possible degree. Their *wages* will be *limited* by the *values* of the products, but the *values of their products* will not be limited by the wages. And above all, the values, the relative values of corn and gold, for example, will have been settled without any regard whatever to the value of the labour employed, that is to say, to *wages*. To determine the values of commodities by the *relative quantities of labour fixed in them*, is, therefore, a thing quite different from the tautological method of determining the values of commodities by the value of labour, or by

[a] A quarter is about 291 litres, while a bushel is about 17 litres, i.e. 1/22nd of a quarter. [Ed.]

wages. This point, however, will be further elucidated in the progress of our inquiry.

In calculating the exchangeable value of a commodity we must add to the quantity of labour *last* employed the quantity of labour *previously* worked up in the raw material of the commodity, and the labour bestowed on the implements, tools, machinery, and buildings, with which such labour is assisted. For example, the value of a certain amount of cotton-yarn is the crystallisation of the quantity of labour added to the cotton during the spinning process, the quantity of labour previously realised in the cotton itself, the quantity of labour realised in the coal, oil and other auxiliary substances used, the quantity of labour fixed in the steam engine, the spindles, the factory building, and so forth. Instruments of production properly so-called, such as tools, machinery, buildings, serve again and again for a longer or shorter period during repeated processes of production. If they were used up at once, like the raw material, their whole value would at once be transferred to the commodities they assist in producing. But as a spindle, for example, is but gradually used up, an average calculation is made, based upon the average time it lasts, and its average waste or wear and tear during a certain period, say a day. In this way we calculate how much of the value of the spindle is transferred to the yarn daily spun, and how much, therefore, of the total amount of labour realised in a pound of yarn, for example, is due to the quantity of labour previously realised in the spindle. For our present purpose it is not necessary to dwell any longer upon this point.

It might seem that if the value of a commodity is determined by the *quantity of labour bestowed upon its production*, the lazier a man, or the clumsier a man, the more valuable his commodity, because the greater the time of labour required for finishing the commodity. This, however, would be a sad mistake. You will recollect that I used the word "*Social* labour", and many points are involved in this qualification of "*Social*". In saying that the value of a commodity is determined by the *quantity of labour* worked up or crystallised in it, we mean *the quantity of labour necessary* for its production in a given state of society, under certain social average conditions of production, with a given social average intensity, and average skill of the labour employed. When, in England, the power-loom came to compete with the hand-loom, only one half of the former time of labour was wanted to convert a given amount of yarn into a yard of cotton or cloth. The poor hand-loom weaver now worked seventeen or eighteen hours daily, instead of the nine or ten hours he had worked before. Still the product of twenty hours of his labour represented now only ten social hours of labour, or ten hours of labour socially necessary for the conversion of a certain amount of yarn into textile stuffs. His product of twenty hours had, therefore, no more value than his former product of ten hours.

If then the quantity of socially necessary labour realised in commodities regulates their exchangeable values, every increase in the quantity of labour wanted for the production of a commodity must augment its value, as every diminution must lower it.

If the respective quantities of labour necessary for the production of the respective commodities remained constant, their relative values also would be constant. But such is not the case. The quantity of labour necessary for the production of a commodity changes continuously with the changes in the productive powers of the labour employed. The greater the productive powers of labour, the more produce is finished in a given time of labour, and the smaller the productive powers of labour, the less produce is finished in the same time. If, for example, in the progress of population it should become necessary to cultivate less fertile soils, the same amount of produce would be only attainable by a greater amount of labour spent, and the value of agricultural produce would consequently rise. On the other hand, if with the modern means of production, a single spinner converts into yarn, during one working day, many thousand times the amount of cotton which he could have spun during the same time with the spinning wheel, it is evident that every single pound of cotton will absorb many thousand times less of spinning labour than it did before, and, consequently, the value added by spinning to every single pound of cotton will be a thousand times less than before. The value of yarn will sink accordingly.

Apart from the different natural energies and acquired working abilities of different peoples, the productive powers of labour must principally depend:

Firstly. Upon the *natural* conditions of labour, such as fertility of soil, mines, and so forth;

Secondly. Upon the progressive improvement of the *Social Powers of Labour*, such as are derived from production on a grand scale, concentration of capital and combination of labour, subdivision of labour, machinery, improved methods, appliance of chemical and other natural agencies, shortening of time and space by means of communication and transport, and every other contrivance by which science presses natural agencies into the service of labour, and by which the social or co-operative character of labour is developed. The greater the productive powers of labour, the less labour is bestowed upon a given amount of produce; hence the smaller the value of this produce. The smaller the productive powers of labour, the more labour is bestowed upon the same amount of produce; hence the greater its value. As a general law we may, therefore, set it down that:

The values of commodities are directly as the times of labour employed in their production, and are inversely as the productive powers of the labour employed.

Having till now only spoken of *Value*, I shall add a few words about *Price*, which is a peculiar form assumed by value.

Price, taken by itself, is nothing but the *monetary expression of value*. The values of all commodities of this country, for example, are expressed in gold prices, while on the Continent they are mainly expressed in silver prices. The value of gold or silver, like that of all other commodities, is regulated by the quantity of labour necessary for getting them. You exchange a certain amount of your national products, in which a certain amount of your national labour is crystallised, for the produce of the gold and silver producing countries, in which a certain quantity of *their* labour is crystallised. It is in this way, in fact by barter, that you learn to express in gold and silver the values of all commodities, that is, the respective quantities of labour bestowed upon them. Looking somewhat closer into the *monetary expression of value*, or what comes to the same, the *conversion of value into price*, you will find that it is a process by which you give to the *values* of all commodities an *independent* and *homogeneous form*, or by which you express them as quantities of *equal* social labour. So far as it is but the monetary expression of value, price has been called *natural price* by Adam Smith, "*prix nécessaire*" by the French physiocrats.

What then is the relation between *value* and *market prices*, or between *natural prices* and *market prices*? You all know that the *market price* is the *same* for all commodities of the same kind, however the conditions of production may differ for the individual producers. The market price expresses only the *average amount of social labour* necessary, under the average conditions of production, to supply the market with a certain mass of a certain article. It is calculated upon the whole lot of a commodity of a certain description.

So far the *market price* of a commodity coincides with its *value*. On the other hand, the oscillations of market prices, rising now over, sinking now under the value or natural price, depend upon the fluctuations of supply and demand. The deviations of market prices from values are continual, but as *Adam Smith* says: "The natural price is ... the central price, to which the prices of all commodities are continually gravitating. Different accidents may sometimes keep them suspended a good deal above it, and sometimes force them down even somewhat below it. But whatever may be the obstacles which hinder them from settling in this centre of repose and continuance, they are constantly tending towards it."

I cannot now sift this matter. It suffices to say that *if* supply and demand equilibrate each other, the market prices of commodities will correspond to their natural prices, that is to say, to their values, as determined by the respective quantities of labour required for their production. But supply and demand *must* constantly tend to equilibrate each other, although they do so only by compensating one fluctuation by another, a rise by a fall, and vice versa. If instead of considering only the daily fluctuations you analyse the movement of market prices for longer periods, as Mr. Tooke, for example, has done in his *History of Prices*, you will find that the fluctuations of market prices, their deviations from values, their ups and downs, paralyse and compensate each other; so that, apart from the effect of monopolies and some other modifications I must now pass by, all descriptions of commodities are, on the average, sold at their respective *values* or natural prices. The average periods during which the fluctuations of market prices compensate each other are different for different kinds of commodities, because with one kind it is easier to adapt supply to demand than with the other.

If then, speaking broadly, and embracing somewhat longer periods, all descriptions of commodities sell at their respective values, it is nonsense to suppose that profit, not in individual cases, but that the constant and usual profits of different trades, spring from surcharging the prices of commodities, or selling them at a price over and above their *value*. The absurdity of this notion becomes evident if it is generalised. What a man would constantly win as a seller he would as constantly lose as a purchaser. It would not do to say that there are men who are buyers without being sellers, or consumers without being producers. What these people pay to the producers, they must first get from them for nothing. If a man first takes your money and afterwards returns that money in buying your commodities, you will never enrich yourselves by selling your commodities too dear to that same man. This sort of transaction might diminish a loss, but would never help in realising a profit.

To explain, therefore, the *general nature of profits*, you must start from the theorem that, on an average, commodities are *sold at their real value*, and that *profits are derived from selling them at their values*, that is, in proportion to the quantity of labour realised in them. If you cannot explain profit upon this supposition, you cannot explain it at all. This seems paradox and contrary to everyday observation. It is also paradox that the earth moves round the sun, and that water consists of two highly inflammable gases. Scientific truth is always paradox, if judged by everyday experience, which catches only the delusive appearance of things.

7) Labouring Power

Having now, as far as it could be done in such a cursory manner, analysed the nature of *Value*, of the *Value of any commodity whatever*, we must turn our attention to the specific *Value of Labour*. And here, again, I must startle you by a seeming paradox. All of you feel sure that what they daily sell is their Labour; that, therefore, Labour has a Price, and that, the price of a commodity being only the monetary expression of its value, there must certainly exist such a thing as the *Value of Labour*. However, there exists no such thing as the *Value of Labour* in the common acceptance of the word. We have seen that the amount of necessary labour crystallised in a commodity constitutes its value. Now, applying this notion of value, how could we define, say, the value of a ten hours' working day? How much labour is contained in that day? Ten hours' labour. To say that the value of a ten hours' working day is equal to ten hours' labour, or the quantity of labour contained in it, would be a tautological and, moreover, a nonsensical expression. Of course, having once found out the true but hidden sense of the expression "*Value of Labour*", we shall be able to interpret this irrational, and seemingly impossible application of value, in the same way that, having once made sure of the real movement of the celestial bodies, we shall be able to explain their apparent or merely phenomenal movements.

What the working man sells is not directly his *Labour*, but his *Labouring Power*, the temporary disposal of which he makes over to the capitalist. This is so much the case that I do not know whether by the English Laws, but certainly by some Continental Laws, the *maximum time* is fixed for which a man is allowed to sell his labouring power. If allowed to do so for any indefinite period whatever, slavery would be immediately restored. Such a sale, if it comprised his lifetime, for example, would make him at once the lifelong slave of his employer.

One of the oldest economists and most original philosophers of England – Thomas Hobbes – has already, in his *Leviathan*, instinctively hit upon this point overlooked by all his successors. He says: "*The value* or *worth of a man* is, as in all other things, his *price*: that is, so much as would be given for the *Use of his Power*."

Proceeding from this basis, we shall be able to determine the *Value of Labour* as that of all other commodities.

But before doing so, we might ask, how does this strange phenomenon arise, that we find on the market a set of buyers, possessed of land, machinery, raw material, and the means of subsistence, all of them, save land in its crude state, the *products of labour*, and on the other hand, a set of sellers who have nothing to sell except their labouring power, their working arms and brains? That the one set buys continually in order to make a profit and enrich themselves, while the other set continually sells in order to earn their livelihood? The inquiry into this question would be an inquiry into what the economists call "*Previous*, or *Original Accumulation*", but which ought to be called *Original Expropriation*. We should find that this so-called *Original Accumulation* means nothing but a series of historical processes, resulting in a *Decomposition of the Original Union* existing between the Labouring Man and his Instruments of Labour. Such an inquiry, however, lies beyond the pale of my present subject. The *Separation* between the Man of Labour and the Instruments of Labour once established, such a state of things will maintain itself and reproduce itself upon a constantly increasing scale, until a new and fundamental revolution in the mode of production should again overturn it, and restore the original union in a new historical form.

What, then, is the *Value of Labouring Power*?

Like that of every other commodity, its value is determined by the quantity of labour necessary to produce it. The labouring power of a man exists only in his living individuality. A certain mass of necessaries must be consumed by a man to grow up and maintain his life. But the man, like the machine, will wear out, and must be replaced by another man. Beside the mass of necessaries required for *his own* maintenance, he wants another amount of necessaries to bring up a certain quota of children that are to replace him on the labour market and to perpetuate the race of labourers. Moreover, to develop his labouring power, and acquire a given skill, another amount of values must be spent. For our purpose it suffices to consider only *average* labour, the costs of whose education and development are vanishing magnitudes. Still I must seize upon this occasion to state that, as the costs of producing labouring powers of different quality differ, so must differ the values of the labouring powers employed in different trades. The cry for an *equality of wages* rests, therefore, upon a mistake, is an *insane* wish never to be fulfilled. It is an offspring of that false and superficial radicalism that accepts premises and tries to evade conclusions. Upon the basis of the wages system the value of labouring power is settled like that of every other commodity; and as different kinds of labouring power have different values, or require different quantities of labour for their production, they *must* fetch different prices in the labour market. To clamour for *equal or even equitable retribution* on the basis of the wages system is the same as to clamour for *freedom* on the basis of the slavery system. What you think just or equitable is out of the question. The question is: What is necessary and unavoidable with a given system of production?

After what has been said, it will be seen that the *value of labouring power* is determined by the *value of the necessaries* required to produce, develop, maintain, and perpetuate the labouring power.

8) Production of Surplus-Value

Now suppose that the average amount of the daily necessaries of a labouring man require *six hours of average labour* for their production. Suppose, moreover, six hours of average labour to be also realised in a quantity of gold equal to 3s. Then 3s. would be the *Price*, or the monetary expression of the *Daily Value* of that man's *Labouring Power*. If he worked daily six hours he would daily produce a value sufficient to buy the average amount of his daily necessaries, or to maintain himself as a labouring man.

But our man is a wages labourer. He must, therefore, sell his labouring power to a capitalist. If he sells it at 3s. daily, or 18s. weekly, he sells it at its value. Suppose him to be a spinner. If he works six hours daily he will add to the cotton a value of 3s. daily. This value, daily added by him, would be an exact equivalent for the wages, or the price of his labouring power, received daily. But in that case *no surplus-value* or *surplus-produce* whatever would go to the capitalist. Here, then, we come to the rub.

In buying the labouring power of the workman, and paying its value, the capitalist, like every other purchaser, has acquired the right to consume or use the commodity bought. You consume or use the labouring power of a man by making him work as you consume or use a machine by making it run. By paying the daily or weekly value of the labouring power of the workman, the capitalist has, therefore, acquired the right to use or make that labouring power work during the *whole day or week*. The working day or the working week has, of course, certain limits, but those we shall afterwards look more closely at.

For the present I want to turn your attention to one decisive point.

The *value* of the labouring power is determined by the quantity of labour necessary to maintain or reproduce it, but the use of that labouring power is only limited by the active energies and physical strength of the labourer. The daily or weekly *value* of the labouring power is quite distinct from the daily or weekly exercise of that power, the same as the food a horse wants and the time it can carry the horseman are quite distinct. The quantity of labour by which the value of the workman's labouring power is limited forms by no means a limit to the quantity of labour which his labouring power is apt to perform. Take the example of our spinner. We have seen that, to daily reproduce his labouring power, he must daily reproduce a value of three shillings, which he will do by working six hours daily. But this does not disable him from working ten or twelve or more hours a day. But by paying the daily or weekly *value* of the spinner's labouring power, the capitalist has acquired the right of using that labouring power during the *whole day or week*. He will, therefore, make him work daily, say, *twelve* hours. *Over and above* the six hours required to replace his wages, or the value of his labouring power, he will, therefore, have to work six other hours, which I shall call hours of *surplus-labour*, which surplus labour will realise itself in a *surplus-value* and a *surplus-produce*. If our spinner, for example, by his daily labour of six hours, added three shillings' value to the cotton, a value forming an exact equivalent to his wages, he will, in twelve hours, add six shillings' worth to the cotton, and produce *a proportional surplus of yarn*. As he has sold his labouring power to the capitalist, the whole value or produce created by him belongs to the capitalist, the owner *pro tempore* of his labouring power. By advancing three shillings, the capitalist will, therefore, realise a value of six shillings, because, advancing a value in which six hours of labour are crystallised, he will receive in return a value in which twelve hours of labour are crystallised. By repeating this same process daily, the capitalist will daily advance three shillings and daily pocket six shillings, one-half of which will go to pay wages anew, and the other half of which will form *surplus-value*, for which the capitalist pays no equivalent. It is *this sort of exchange between capital and labour* upon which capitalistic production, or the wages system, is founded, and which must constantly result in reproducing the working man as a working man, and the capitalist as a capitalist.

The rate of surplus-value, all other circumstances remaining the same, will depend on the proportion between that part of the working day necessary to reproduce the value of the labouring power and the *surplus-time* or *surplus-labour* performed for the capitalist. It will, therefore, depend on the *ratio in which the working day is prolonged over and above that extent,* by working which the working man would only reproduce the value of his labouring power, or replace his wages.

9) Value of Labour

We must now return to the expression, "*Value, or Price of Labour*".

We have seen that, in fact, it is only the value of the labouring power, measured by the values of commodities necessary for its maintenance. But since the workman receives his wages after his labour is performed, and knows, moreover, that what he actually gives to the capitalist is his labour, the value or price of his labouring power necessarily appears to him as the *price or value of his labour itself*. If the price of his labouring power is three shillings, in which six hours of labour are realised, and if he works twelve hours, he necessarily considers these three shillings as the value or price of twelve hours of labour, although these twelve hours of labour realise themselves in a value of six shillings. A double consequence flows from this.

Firstly. The value or price of the labouring power takes the semblance of the *price or value of labour itself*, although, strictly speaking, value and price of labour are senseless terms.

Secondly. Although one part only of the workman's daily labour is *paid*, while the other part is *unpaid*, and while that unpaid or surplus-labour constitutes exactly the fund out of which *surplus-value* or *profit* is formed, it seems as if the aggregate labour was paid labour.

This false appearance distinguishes *wages labour* from other *historical* forms of labour. On the basis of the wages system even the *unpaid* labour seems to be *paid* labour. With the *slave*, on the contrary, even that part of his labour which is paid appears to be unpaid. Of course, in order to work the slave must live, and one part of his working day goes to replace the value of his own maintenance. But since no bargain is struck between him and his master, and no acts of selling and buying are going on between the two parties, all his labour seems to be given away for nothing.

Take, on the other hand, the peasant serf, such as he, I might say, until yesterday existed in the whole East of Europe. This peasant worked, for example, three days for himself on his own field or the field allotted to him, and the three subsequent days he performed compulsory and gratuitous labour on the estate of his lord. Here, then, the paid and unpaid parts of labour were visibly separated, separated in time and space; and our Liberals overflowed with moral indignation at the preposterous notion of making a man work for nothing.

In point of fact, however, whether a man works three days of the week for himself on his own field and three days for nothing on the estate of his lord, or whether he works in the factory or the workshop six hours daily for himself and six for his employer, comes to the same, although in the latter case the paid and unpaid portions of labour are inseparably mixed up with each other, and the nature of the whole transaction is completely masked by the *intervention of a contract* and the *pay* received at the end of the week. The gratuitous labour appears to be voluntarily given in the one instance, and to be compulsory in the other. That makes all the difference.

In using the expression "*value of labour*", I shall only use it as a popular slang term for "*value of labouring power*".

10) Profit is Made by Selling a Commodity *at* Its Value

Suppose an average hour of labour to be realised in a value equal to sixpence, or twelve average hours of labour to be realised in six shillings. Suppose, further, the value of labour to be three shillings or the produce of six hours' labour. If, then, in the raw material, machinery, and so forth, used up in a commodity, twenty-four hours of average labour were realised, its value would amount to twelve shillings. If, moreover, the workman employed by the capitalist added twelve hours of labour to those means of production, these twelve hours would be realised in an additional value of six shillings. The *total value of the product* would, therefore, amount to thirty-six hours of realised labour, and be equal to eighteen shillings. But as the value of labour, or the wages paid to the workman, would be three shillings only, no equivalent would have been paid by the capitalist for the six hours of surplus-labour worked by the workman, and realised in the value of the commodity. By selling this commodity at its value for eighteen shillings, the capitalist would, therefore, realise a value of three shillings, for which he had paid no equivalent. These three shillings would constitute the surplus-value or profit pocketed by him. The capitalist would consequently realise the profit of three shillings, not by selling his commodity at a price *over and above* its value, but by selling it *at its real value.*

The value of a commodity is determined by the *total quantity of labour* contained in it. But part of that quantity of labour is realised in a value for which an equivalent has been paid in the form of wages; part of it is realised in a value for which *no* equivalent has been paid. Part of the labour contained in the commodity is *paid* labour; part is *unpaid* labour. By selling, therefore, the commodity *at its value*, that is, as the crystallisation of the *total quantity of labour* bestowed upon it, the capitalist must necessarily sell it at a profit. He sells not only what has cost him an equivalent, but he sells also what has cost him nothing, although it has cost his workman labour. The cost of the commodity to the capitalist and its real cost are different things. I repeat, therefore, that normal and average profits are made by selling commodities not *above* but *at their real values.*

11) The Different Parts into Which Surplus-Value is Decomposed

The *surplus-value*, or that part of the total value of the commodity in which the *surplus-labour* or *unpaid labour* of the working man is realised, I call *Profit.* The whole of that profit is not pocketed by the employing capitalist. The monopoly of land enables the landlord to take one part of that *surplus-value*, under the name of *rent*, whether the land is used for agriculture, buildings or railways, or for any other productive purpose. On the other hand, the very fact that the possession of the *means of labour* enables the employing capitalist to produce a *surplus-value*, or, what comes to the same, to *appropriate to himself a certain amount of unpaid labour*, enables the owner of the means of labour, which he lends wholly or partly to the employing capitalist – enables, in one word, the *money-lending capitalist* to claim for himself under the name of *interest* another part of that surplus-value, so that there remains to the employing capitalist *as such* only what is called *industrial* or *commercial profit.*

By what laws this division of the total amount of surplus-value amongst the three categories of people is regulated is a question quite foreign to our subject. This much, however, results from what has been stated.

Rent, Interest, and Industrial Profit are only *different names for different parts* of the *surplus-value* of the commodity, or the *unpaid labour enclosed in it*, and they are *equally derived from this source, and from this source alone.* They are not derived from *land* as such or from *capital* as such, but land and capital enable their owners to get their respective shares out of the surplus-value extracted by the employing capitalist from the labourer. For the labourer himself it is a matter of subordinate importance whether that surplus-value, the result of his surplus-labour, or unpaid labour, is altogether pocketed by the employing capitalist, or whether the latter is obliged to pay portions of it, under the name of rent and interest, away to third parties. Suppose the employing capitalist to use only his own capital and to be his own landlord, then the whole surplus-value would go into his pocket.

It is the employing capitalist who immediately extracts from the labourer this surplus-value, whatever part of it he may ultimately be able to keep for himself. Upon this relation, therefore, between the employing capitalist and the wages labourer the whole wages system and the whole present system of production hinge. Some of the citizens who took part in our debate were, therefore, wrong in trying to mince matters, and to treat this fundamental relation between the employing capitalist and the working man as a secondary question, although they were right in stating that, under given circumstances, a rise of prices might affect in very unequal degrees the employing capitalist, the landlord, the moneyed capitalist, and, if you please, the tax-gatherer.

Another consequence follows from what has been stated.

That part of the value of the commodity which represents only the value of the raw materials, the machinery, in one word, the value of the means of production used up, forms no revenue at all, but replaces *only capital*. But, apart from this, it is false that the other part of the value of the commodity *which forms revenue*, or may be spent in the form of wages, profits, rent, interest, is *constituted* by the value of wages, the value of rent, the value of profits, and so forth. We shall, in the first instance, discard wages, and only treat industrial profits, interest, and rent. We have just seen that the *surplus-value* contained in the commodity or that part of its value in which *unpaid labour* is realised, *dissolves* itself into different fractions, bearing three different names. But it would be quite the reverse of the truth to say that its value is *composed* of, or *formed* by, the *addition* of the *independent values of these three constituents.*

If one hour of labour realises itself in a value of sixpence, if the working day of the labourer comprises twelve hours, if half of this time is unpaid labour, that surplus-labour will add to the commodity a *surplus-value* of three shillings, that is, a value for which no equivalent has been paid. This surplus-value of three shillings constitutes the *whole fund* which the employing capitalist may divide, in whatever proportions, with the landlord and the money-lender. The value of these three shillings constitutes the limit of the value they have to divide amongst them. But it is not the employing capitalist who adds to the value of the commodity an arbitrary value for his profit, to which another value is added for the landlord and so forth, so that the addition of these arbitrarily fixed values would constitute the total value. You see, therefore, the fallacy of the popular notion, which confounds the *decomposition of a given value* into three parts, with the *formation* of that value by the addition of three *independent* values, thus converting the aggregate value, from which rent, profit, and interest are derived, into an arbitrary magnitude.

If the total profit realised by a capitalist be equal to £100, we call this sum, considered as *absolute* magnitude, the *amount of profit*. But if we calculate the ratio which those £100 bear to the capital advanced, we call this *relative* magnitude, the *rate of profit*. It is evident that this rate of profit may be expressed in a double way.

Suppose £100 to be the capital *advanced in wages*. If the surplus value created is also £100 – and this would show us that half the working day of the labourer consists of unpaid labour – and if we measured this profit by the value of the capital advanced in wages, we should say that the *rate of profit* amounted to one hundred per cent., because the value advanced would be one hundred and the value realised would be two hundred.

If, on the other hand, we should not only consider the *capital advanced in wages*, but the *total capital* advanced, say for example £500, of which £400 represented the value of raw materials, machinery, and so forth, we should say that the *rate of profit* amounted only to twenty per cent., because the profit of one hundred would be but the fifth part of the *total* capital advanced.

The first mode of expressing the rate of profit is the only one which shows you the real ratio between paid and unpaid labour, the real degree of the *exploitation* (you must allow me this French word) *of labour*. The other mode of expression is that in common use, and is, indeed, appropriate for certain purposes. At all events, it is very useful for concealing the degree in which the capitalist extracts gratuitous labour from the workman.

In the remarks I have still to make I shall use the word *Profit* for the whole amount of the surplus-value extracted by the capitalist without any regard to the division of the surplus-value between different parties, and in using the words *Rate of Profit*, I shall always measure profits by the value of the capital advanced in wages.

12) General Relation of Profits, Wages and Prices

Deduct from the value of a commodity the value replacing the value of the raw materials and other means of production used upon it, that is to say, deduct the value representing the *past* labour contained in it, and the remainder of its value will dissolve into the quantity of labour added by the working man *last* employed. If that working man works twelve hours daily, if twelve hours of average labour crystallise themselves in an amount of gold equal to six shillings, this additional value of six shillings is the *only* value his labour will have created. This given value, determined by the time of his labour, is the only fund from which both he and the capitalist have to draw their respective shares or dividends, the only value to be divided into wages and profits. It is evident that this value itself will not be altered by the variable proportions in which it may be divided amongst the two parties. There will also be nothing changed if in the place of one working man you put the whole working population, twelve million working days, for example, instead of one.

Since the capitalist and workman have only to divide this limited value, that is, the value measured by the total labour of the working man, the more the one gets the less will the other get, and vice versa. Whenever a quantity is given, one part of it will increase inversely as the other decreases. If the wages change, profits will change in an opposite direction. If wages fall, profits will rise; and if wages rise, profits will fall. If the working man, on our former supposition, gets three shillings, equal to one half of the value he has created, or if his whole working day consists half of paid, half of unpaid labour, the *rate of profit* will be 100 per cent., because the capitalist would also get three shillings. If the working man receives only two shillings, or works only one-third of the whole day for himself, the capitalist will get four shillings, and the rate of profit will be 200 per cent. If the working man receives four shillings, the capitalist will only receive two, and the rate of profit would sink to 50 per cent., but all these variations will not affect the value of the commodity. A general rise of wages would, therefore, result in a fall of the general rate of profit, but not affect values.

But although the values of commodities, which must ultimately regulate their market prices, are exclusively determined by the total quantities of labour fixed in them, and not by the division of that quantity into paid and unpaid labour, it by no means follows that the values of the single commodities, or lots of commodities, produced during twelve hours, for example, will remain constant. The *number* or mass of commodities produced in a given time of labour, or by a given quantity of labour, depends upon the *productive power* of the labour employed, and not upon its *extent* or length. With one degree of the productive power of spinning labour, for example, a working day of twelve hours may produce twelve pounds of yarn, with a lesser degree of productive power only two pounds. If then twelve hours' average labour were realised in the value of six shillings, in the one case the twelve pounds of yarn would cost six shillings, in the other case the two pounds of yarn would also cost six shillings. One pound of yarn would, therefore, cost sixpence in the one case, and three shillings in the other. This difference of price would result from the difference in the productive powers of the labour employed. One hour of labour would be realised in one pound of yarn with the greater productive power, while with the smaller productive power, six hours of labour would be realised in one pound of yarn. The price of a pound of yarn would, in the one instance, be only sixpence, although wages were relatively high and the rate of profit low; it would be three shillings in the other instance, although wages were low and the rate of profit high. This would be so because the price of the pound of yarn is regulated by the *total amount of labour worked up* in it, and not by the *proportional division of that total amount into paid and unpaid labour*. The fact I have before mentioned that high-priced labour may produce cheap, and low-priced labour may produce dear commodities, loses, therefore, its paradoxical appearance. It is only the expression of the general law that the value of a commodity is regulated by the quantity of labour worked up in it, and that the quantity of labour worked up in it depends altogether upon the productive powers of the labour employed, and will, therefore, vary with every variation in the productivity of labour.

13) Main Cases of Attempts at Rising Wages or Resisting Their Fall

Let us now seriously consider the main cases in which a rise of wages is attempted or a reduction of wages resisted.

1. We have seen that the *value of the labouring power*, or in more popular parlance, the *value of labour*, is determined by the value of necessaries, or the quantity of labour required to produce them. If, then, in a given country the value of the daily average necessaries of the labourer represented six hours of labour expressed in three shillings, the labourer would have to work six hours daily to produce an equivalent for his daily maintenance. If the whole working day was twelve hours, the capitalist would pay him the value of his labour by paying him three shillings. Half the working day would be unpaid labour, and the rate of profit would amount to 100 per cent. But now suppose that, consequent upon a decrease of productivity, more labour should be wanted to produce, say, the same amount of agricultural produce, so that the price of the average daily necessaries should rise from three to four shillings. In that case the *value* of labour would rise by one-third, or 33⅓ per cent. Eight

hours of the working day would be required to produce an equivalent for the daily maintenance of the labourer, according to his old standard of living. The surplus-labour would therefore sink from six hours to four, and the rate of profit from 100 to 50 per cent. But in insisting upon a rise of wages, the labourer would only insist upon getting the *increased value of his labour*, like every other seller of a commodity, who, the costs of his commodities having increased, tries to get its increased value paid. If wages did not rise, or not sufficiently rise, to compensate for the increased values of necessaries, the *price* of labour would sink *below the value of labour*, and the labourer's standard of life would deteriorate.

But a change might also take place in an opposite direction. By virtue of the increased productivity of labour, the same amount of the average daily necessaries might sink from three to two shillings, or only four hours out of the working day, instead of six, be wanted to reproduce an equivalent for the value of the daily necessaries. The working man would now be able to buy with two shillings as many necessaries as he did before with three shillings. Indeed, the *value of labour* would have sunk, but that diminished value would command the same amount of commodities as before. Then profits would rise from three to four shillings, and, the rate of profit from 100 to 200 per cent. Although the labourer's absolute standard of life would have remained the same, his relative wages, and therewith his *relative social position*, as compared with that of the capitalist, would have been lowered. If the working man should resist that reduction of relative wages, he would only try to get some share in the increased productive powers of his own labour, and to maintain his former relative position in the social scale. Thus, after the abolition of the Corn Laws, and in flagrant violation of the most solemn pledges given during the anti-corn law agitation, the English factory lords generally reduced wages ten per cent. The resistance of the workmen was at first baffled, but, consequent upon circumstances I cannot now enter upon, the ten per cent. lost were afterwards regained.

2. The *values* of necessaries, and consequently the *value of labour*, might remain the same, but a change might occur in their *money prices*, consequent upon a previous *change* in the *value of money*.

By the discovery of more fertile mines and so forth, two ounces of gold might, for example, cost no more labour to produce than one ounce did before. The *value* of gold would then be depreciated by one half, or fifty per cent. As the *values* of all other commodities would then be expressed in twice their former *money prices*, so also the same with the *value of labour*. Twelve hours of labour, formerly expressed in six shillings, would now be expressed in twelve shillings. If the working man's wages should remain three shillings, instead of rising to six shillings, the *money price of his labour* would only be equal to *half the value of his labour*, and his standard of life would fearfully deteriorate. This would also happen in a greater or lesser degree if his wages should rise, but not proportionately to the fall in the value of gold. In such a case nothing would have been changed, either in the productive powers of labour, or in supply and demand, or in values. Nothing could have changed except the money *names* of those values. To say that in such a case the workman ought not to insist upon a proportionate rise of wages, is to say that he must be content to be paid with names, instead of with things. All past history proves that whenever such a depreciation of money occurs the capitalists are on the alert to seize this opportunity for defrauding the workman. A very large school of political economists assert that, consequent upon the new discoveries of gold lands, the better working of silver mines, and the cheaper supply of quicksilver, the value of precious metals has been again depreciated. This would explain the general and simultaneous attempts on the Continent at a rise of wages.

3. We have till now supposed that the *working day* has given limits. The working day, however, has, by itself, no constant limits. It is the constant tendency of capital to stretch it to its utmost physically possible length, because in the same degree surplus-labour, and consequently the profit resulting therefrom, will be increased. The more capital succeeds in

prolonging the working day, the greater the amount of other people's labour it will appropriate. During the seventeenth and even the first two-thirds of the eighteenth century a ten hours' working day was the normal working day all over England. During the anti-Jacobin war, which was in fact a war waged by the British barons against the British working masses capital celebrated its bacchanalia, and prolonged the working day from ten to twelve, fourteen, eighteen hours. *Malthus*, by no means a man whom you would suspect of a maudlin sentimentalism, declared in a pamphlet, published about 1815, that if this sort of things was to go on the life of the nation would be attacked at its very source. A few years before the general introduction of the newly-invented machinery, about 1765, a pamphlet appeared in England under the title, *An Essay on Trade*. The anonymous author, an avowed enemy of the working classes, declaims on the necessity of expanding the limits of the working day. Amongst other means to this end, he proposes *working houses*, which, he says, ought to be "*Houses of Terror*". And what is the length of the working day he prescribes for these "*Houses of Terror*"? *Twelve hours*, the very same time which in 1832 was declared by capitalists, political economists, and ministers to be not only the existing but the necessary time of labour for a child under twelve years.[a]

By selling his labouring power, and he must do so under the present system, the working man makes over to the capitalist the consumption of that power, but within certain rational limits. He sells his labouring power in order to maintain it, apart from its natural wear and tear, but not to destroy it. In selling his labouring power at its daily or weekly value, it is understood that in one day or one week that labouring power shall not be submitted to two days' or two weeks' waste or wear and tear. Take a machine worth £1,000. If it is used up in ten years it will add to the value of the commodities in whose production it assists £100 yearly.

[a] A reference to the stand taken by the representatives of British capitalist and official circles when the Ten Hours' Bill of 1831 for children and adolescents was debated in Parliament in February and March 1832. [Ed.]

If it be used up in five years it would add £200 yearly, or the value of its annual wear and tear is in inverse ratio to the quickness with which it is consumed. But this distinguishes the working man from the machine. Machinery does not wear out exactly in the same ratio in which it is used. Man, on the contrary, decays in a greater ratio than would be visible from the mere numerical addition of work.

In their attempts at reducing the working day to its former rational dimensions, or, where they cannot enforce a legal fixation of a normal working day, at checking overwork by a rise of wages, a rise not only in proportion to the surplus-time exacted, but in a greater proportion, working men fulfil only a duty to themselves and their race. They only set limits to the tyrannical usurpations of capital. Time is the room of human development. A man who has no free time to dispose of, whose whole lifetime, apart from the mere physical interruptions by sleep, meals, and so forth, is absorbed by his labour for the capitalist, is less than a beast of burden. He is a mere machine for producing Foreign Wealth, broken in body and brutalised in mind. Yet the whole history of modern industry shows that capital, if not checked, will recklessly and ruthlessly work to cast down the whole working class to the utmost state of degradation.

In prolonging the working day the capitalist may pay *higher wages* and still lower the *value of labour*, if the rise of wages does not correspond to the greater amount of labour extracted, and the quicker decay of the labouring power thus caused. This may be done in another way. Your middle-class statisticians will tell you, for instance, that the average wages of factory families in Lancashire have risen. They forget that instead of the labour of the man, the head of the family, his wife and perhaps three or four children are now thrown under the Juggernaut wheels [a] of capital, and that the rise of

[a] Juggernaut – a title of Krishna, the eighth avatar of Vishnu. The cult of Juggernaut was marked by sumptuous ritual and extreme fanaticism which included self-torture and suicide of believers. On feast day some believers threw themselves under the wheels of the chariot bearing the idol of Vishnu-Juggernaut. [Ed.]

the aggregate wages does not correspond to the aggregate surplus-labour extracted from the family.

Even with given limits of the working day, such as now exist in all branches of industry subjected to the factory laws, a rise of wages may become necessary, if only to keep up the old standard *value of labour*. By increasing the *intensity* of labour, a man may be made to expend as much vital force in one hour as he formerly did in two. This has, to a certain degree, been effected in the trades, placed under the Factory Acts, by the acceleration of machinery, and the greater number of working machines which a single individual has now to superintend. If the increase in the intensity of labour or the mass of labour spent in an hour keeps some fair proportion to the decrease in the extent of the working day, the working man will still be the winner. If this limit is overshot, he loses in one form what he has gained in another, and ten hours of labour may then become as ruinous as twelve hours were before. In checking this tendency of capital, by struggling for a rise of wages corresponding to the rising intensity of labour, the working man only resists the depreciation of his labour and the deterioration of his race.

4. All of you know that, from reasons I have not now to explain, capitalistic production moves through certain periodical cycles. It moves through a state of quiescence, growing animation, prosperity, overtrade, crisis, and stagnation. The market prices of commodities, and the market rates of profit, follow these phases, now sinking below their averages, now rising above them. Considering the whole cycle, you will find that one deviation of the market price is being compensated by the other, and that, taking the average of the cycle, the market prices of commodities are regulated by their values. Well! During the phase of sinking market prices and the phases of crisis and stagnation, the working man, if not thrown out of employment altogether, is sure to have his wages lowered. Not to be defrauded, he must, even with such a fall of market prices, debate with the capitalist in what proportional degree a fall of wages has become necessary. If, during the phases of

prosperity, when extra profits are made, he did not battle for a rise of wages, he would, taking the average of one industrial cycle, not even receive his *average wages*, or the *value* of his labour. It is the utmost height of folly to demand that while his wages are necessarily affected by the adverse phases of the cycle, he should exclude himself from compensation during the prosperous phases of the cycle. Generally, the *values* of all commodities are only realised by the compensation of the continuously changing market prices, springing from the continuous fluctuations of demand and supply. On the basis of the present system labour is only a commodity like others. It must, therefore, pass through the same fluctuations to fetch an average price corresponding to its value. It would be absurd to treat it on the one hand as a commodity, and to want on the other hand to exempt it from the laws which regulate the prices of commodities. The slave receives a permanent and fixed amount of maintenance; the wages labourer does not. He must try to get a rise of wages in the one instance, if only to compensate for a fall of wages in the other. If he resigned himself to accept the will, the dictates of the capitalist as a permanent economical law, he would share in all the miseries of the slave, without the security of the slave.

5. In all the cases I have considered, and they form ninety-nine out of a hundred, you have seen that a struggle for a rise of wages follows only in the track of *previous* changes, and is the necessary offspring of previous changes in the amount of production, the productive powers of labour, the value of labour, the value of money, the extent or the intensity of labour extracted, the fluctuations of market prices, dependent upon the fluctuations of demand and supply, and consistent with the different phases of the industrial cycle; in one word, as reactions of labour against the previous action of capital. By treating the struggle for a rise of wages independently of all these circumstances, by looking only upon the change of wages, and overlooking all the other changes from which they emanate, you proceed from a false premise in order to arrive at false conclusions.

14) The Struggle Between Capital and Labour and Its Results

1. Having shown that the periodical resistance on the part of the working men against a reduction of wages, and their periodical attempts at getting a rise of wages, are inseparable from the wages system, and dictated by the very fact of labour being assimilated to commodities, and therefore subject to the laws regulating the general movement of prices; having, furthermore, shown that a general rise of wages would result in a fall in the general rate of profit, but not affect the average prices of commodities, or their values, the question now ultimately arises, how far, in this incessant struggle between capital and labour, the latter is likely to prove successful.

I might answer by a generalisation, and say that, as with all other commodities, so with labour, its *market price* will, in the long run, adapt itself to its *value*; that, therefore, despite all the ups and downs, and do what he may, the working man will, on an average, only receive the value of his labour, which resolves into the value of his labouring power, which is determined by the value of the necessaries required for its maintenance and reproduction, which value of necessaries finally is regulated by the quantity of labour wanted to produce them.

But there are some peculiar features which distinguish the *value of the labouring power*, or *the value of labour*, from the values of all other commodities. The value of the labouring power is formed by two elements – the one merely physical, the other historical or social. Its *ultimate limit* is determined by the *physical* element, that is to say, to maintain and reproduce itself, to perpetuate its physical existence, the working class must receive the necessaries absolutely indispensable for living and multiplying. The *value* of those indispensable necessaries forms, therefore, the ultimate limit of the *value of labour.* On the other hand, the length of the working day is also limited by ultimate, although very elastic boundaries. Its ultimate limit is given by the physical force of the labouring man. If the daily exhaustion of his vital forces exceeds a certain degree, it cannot be exerted anew, day by day. However, as I said, this limit is very elastic. A quick succession of unhealthy and short-lived generations will keep the labour market as well supplied as a series of vigorous and long-lived generations.

Besides this mere physical element, the value of labour is in every country determined by a *traditional standard of life.* It is not mere physical life, but it is the satisfaction of certain wants springing from the social conditions in which people are placed and reared up. The English standard of life may be reduced to the Irish standard; the standard of life of a German peasant to that of a Livonian peasant. The important part which historical tradition and social habitude play in this respect, you may learn from Mr. Thornton's work on *Over-population*, where he shows that the average wages in different agricultural districts of England still nowadays differ more or less according to the more or less favourable circumstances under which the districts have emerged from the state of serfdom.

This historical or social element, entering into the value of labour, may be expanded, or contracted; or altogether extinguished, so that nothing remains but the *physical limit.* During the time of the *anti-Jacobin war*, undertaken, as the incorrigible tax-eater and sinecurist, old George Rose, used to say, to save the comforts of our holy religion from the inroads of the French infidels, the honest English farmers, so tenderly handled in a former chapter of ours, depressed the wages of the agricultural labourers even beneath that *mere physical minimum*, but made up by *Poor Laws* the remainder necessary for the physical perpetuation of the race. This was a glorious way to convert the wages labourer into a slave, and Shakespeare's proud yeoman into a pauper.

By comparing the standard wages or values of labour in different countries, and by comparing them in different historical epochs of the same country, you will find that the *value of labour* itself is not a fixed but a variable magnitude, even supposing the values of all other commodities to remain constant.

A similar comparison would prove that not only the *market rates of profit* change but its *average rates.*

But as to *profits,* there exists no law which determines their *minimum.* We cannot say what is the ultimate limit of their decrease. And why cannot we fix that limit? Because, although we can fix the *minimum* of wages, we cannot fix their *maximum.* We can only say that, the limits of the working day being given, the *maximum of profit* corresponds to the *physical minimum of wages*; and that wages being given, the *maximum of profit* corresponds to such a prolongation of the working day as is compatible with the physical forces of the labourer. The maximum of profit is, therefore, limited by the physical minimum of wages and the physical maximum of the working day. It is evident that between the two limits of this *maximum rate of profit* an immense scale of variations is possible. The fixation of its actual degree is only settled by the continuous struggle between capital and labour, the capitalist constantly tending to reduce wages to their physical minimum, and to extend the working day to its physical maximum, while the working man constantly presses in the opposite direction.

The matter resolves itself into a question of the respective powers of the combatants.

2. As to the *limitation of the working day* in England, as in all other countries, it has never been settled except by *legislative interference.* Without the working men's continuous pressure from without that interference would never have taken place. But at all events, the result was not to be attained by private settlement between the working men and the capitalists. This very necessity of *general political action* affords the proof that in its merely economic action capital is the stronger side.

As to the *limits* of the *value of labour,* its actual settlement always depends upon supply and demand. I mean the demand for labour on the part of capital, and the supply of labour by the working men. In colonial countries the law of supply and demand favours the working man. Hence the relatively high standard of wages in the United States. Capital may there try its utmost. It cannot prevent the labour market from being continuously emptied by the continuous conversion of wages labourers into independent, self-sustaining peasants. The position of a wages labourer is for a very large part of the American people but a probational state, which they are sure to leave within a longer or shorter term. To mend this colonial state of things, the paternal British Government accepted for some time what is called the modern colonisation theory, which consists in putting an artificial high price upon colonial land, in order to prevent the too quick conversion of the wages labourer into the independent peasant.

But let us now come to old civilised countries, in which capital domineers over the whole process of production. Take, for example, the rise in England of agricultural wages from 1849 to 1859. What was its consequence? The farmers could not, as our friend Weston would have advised them, raise the value of wheat, nor even its market prices. They had, on the contrary, to submit to their fall. But during these eleven years they introduced machinery of all sorts, adopted more scientific methods, converted part of arable land into pasture, increased the size of farms, and with this the scale of production, and by these and other processes, diminishing the demand for labour by increasing its productive power, made the agricultural population again relatively redundant. This is the general method in which a reaction, quicker or slower, of capital against a rise of wages takes place in old, settled countries. Ricardo has justly remarked that machinery is in constant competition with labour, and can often be only introduced when the price of labour has reached a certain height, but the appliance of machinery is but one of the many methods for increasing the productive powers of labour. This very same development which makes common labour relatively redundant simplifies on the other hand skilled labour, and thus depreciates it.

The same law obtains in another form. With the development of the productive powers of labour the accumulation of capital will be accelerated, even despite a relatively high rate of wages. Hence, one might infer, as *Adam Smith*, in whose days modern industry was still in its infancy, did infer, that the accelerated accumulation of capital must turn the balance in favour of the working man, by securing a growing demand for his labour. From this same standpoint many contemporary writers have wondered that English capital having grown in the last twenty years so much quicker than English population, wages should not have been more enhanced. But simultaneously with the progress of accumulation there takes place a *progressive change* in the *composition of capital*. That part of the aggregate capital which consists of fixed capital, machinery, raw materials, means of production in all possible forms, progressively increases as compared with the other part of capital, which is laid out in wages or in the purchase of labour. This law has been stated in a more or less accurate manner by Mr. Barton, Ricardo, Sismondi, Professor Richard Jones, Professor Ramsay, Cherbuliez, and others.

If the proportion of these two elements of capital was originally one to one, it will, in the progress of industry, become five to one, and so forth. If of a total capital of 600, 300 is laid out in instruments, raw materials, and so forth, and 300 in wages, the total capital wants only to be doubled to create a demand for 600 working men instead of for 300. But if of a capital of 600, 500 is laid out in machinery, materials, and so forth, and 100 only in wages, the same capital must increase from 600 to 3,600 in order to create a demand for 600 workmen instead of 300. In the progress of industry the demand for labour keeps, therefore, no pace with accumulation of capital. It will still increase, but increase in a constantly diminishing ratio as compared with the increase of capital.

These few hints will suffice to show that the very development of modern industry must progressively turn the scale in favour of the capitalist against the working man, and that consequently the general tendency of capitalistic production is not to raise, but to sink the average standard of wages, or to push the *value of labour* more or less to its *minimum limit*. Such being the tendency of *things* in this system, is this saying that the working class ought to renounce their resistance against the encroachments of capital, and abandon their attempts at making the best of the occasional chances for their temporary improvement? If they did, they would be degraded to one level mass of broken wretches past salvation. I think I have shown that their struggles for the standard of wages are incidents inseparable from the whole wages system, that in 99 cases out of 100 their efforts at raising wages are only efforts at maintaining the given value of labour, and that the necessity of debating their price with the capitalist is inherent in their condition of having to sell themselves as commodities. By cowardly giving way in their everyday conflict with capital, they would certainly disqualify themselves for the initiating of any larger movement.

At the same time, and quite apart from the general servitude involved in the wages system, the working class ought not to exaggerate to themselves the ultimate working of these everyday struggles. They ought not to forget that they are fighting with effects, but not with the causes of those effects; that they are retarding the downward movement, but not changing its direction; that they are applying palliatives, not curing the malady. They ought, therefore, not to be exclusively absorbed in these unavoidable guerilla fights incessantly springing up from the never-ceasing encroachments of capital or changes of the market. They ought to understand that, with all the miseries it imposes upon them, the present system simultaneously engenders the *material conditions* and the *social forms* necessary for an economical reconstruction of society. Instead of the *conservative* motto, "*A fair day's wage for a fair day's work!*" they ought to inscribe on their banner the *revolutionary* watchword, "*Abolition of the wages system!*"

After this very long and, I fear, tedious exposition which I was obliged to enter into to do some justice to the subject-matter, I shall conclude by proposing the following resolutions:

Firstly. A general rise in the rate of wages would result in a fall of the general rate of profit, but, broadly speaking, not affect the prices of commodities.

Secondly. The general tendency of capitalist production is not to raise, but to sink the average standard of wages.

Thirdly. Trades Unions work well as centres of resistance against the encroachments of capital. They fail partially from an injudicious use of their power. They fail generally from limiting themselves to a guerilla war against the effects of the existing system, instead of simultaneously trying to change it, instead of using their organised forces as a lever for the final emancipation of the working class, that is to say, the ultimate abolition of the wages system.

Index of Names

Books published by Éditions Science Marxiste

English

Texts

Arrigo Cervetto	CLASS STRUGGLES AND THE REVOLUTIONARY PARTY
Arrigo Cervetto	THE DIFFICULT QUESTION OF TIMES
Arrigo Cervetto	THE POLITICAL SHELL
Arrigo Cervetto	METHOD AND THE SCIENCE-PARTY
Arrigo Cervetto	UNITARY IMPERIALISM, VOLUME I
Arrigo Cervetto	UNITARY IMPERIALISM, VOLUME II
Nicola Capelluto	THE CRISIS IN GLOBAL RELATIONS
Renato Pastorino	THE UNPRECEDENTED TASK
Guido La Barbera	THE NEW STRATEGIC PHASE
Guido La Barbera	LOTTA COMUNISTA : THE ORIGINS 1943-1952
Guido La Barbera	LOTTA COMUNISTA: TOWARDS THE STRATEGY-PARTY 1953-1965
Anthology	REACTIONARY TERRORISM, IMPERIALIST EUROPEANISM, COMMUNIST INTERNATIONALISM

Documents

David B. Rjazanov	THE ORIGINS OF THE FIRST INTERNATIONAL
G. G. CAVICCHIOLI (ed.)	OCTOBER 1917 100 Years, 100 Militants of the Revolution

Publications for young people

Arrigo Cervetto	LENIN AND THE CHINESE REVOLUTION Lenin – Inflammable Material in World Politics and other writings
Friedrich Engels	ANTIDHÜRING & THE ROLE OF FORCE IN HISTORY Arrigo Cervetto – The Discovery of Politics
Vladimir Ilyich Lenin	IMPERIALISM, THE HIGHEST STAGE OF CAPITALISM Arrigo Cervetto – The Marxist Theory of International Relations
Vladimir Ilyich Lenin	STATE AND REVOLUTION Arrigo Cervetto – The Restoration of Marxist Theory
Karl Marx	WAGE LABOUR AND CAPITAL WAGES, PRICE AND PROFIT

Anthology	MAY DAY IN WORKING-CLASS HISTORY Ist May Internationalist Workers' Day
Anthology	THE COMMUNIST CHOICE Understanding the Present, Changing the Future
Anthology	OUR INTERNATIONALIST STRUGGLE The Direction of the New Strategic Phase

French

Collection Textes

Arrigo Cervetto	LA DIFFICILE QUESTION DES TEMPS
Arrigo Cervetto	LUTTES DE CLASSE ET PARTI RÉVOLUTIONNAIRE
Arrigo Cervetto	LE MONDE MULTIPOLAIRE 1990-1995
Arrigo Cervetto	L'ENVELOPPE POLITIQUE
Arrigo Cervetto	MÉTHODE ET PARTI-SCIENCE
Arrigo Cervetto	L'IMPÉRIALISME UNITAIRE Tome I, 1950-1967
Arrigo Cervetto	L'IMPÉR IALISME UNITAIRE Tome II, 1959-1980
Guido La Barbera	LA CRISE DU CAPITALISME D'ÉTAT
Guido La Barbera	L'EUROPE ET LA GUERRE
Guido La Barbera	L'ORDRE INSTABLE DU MULTIPOLARISME
Guido La Barbera	L'EUROPE ET L'ÉTAT
Guido La Barbera	L'EUROPE, L'ASIE ET LA CRISE
Guido La Barbera	CRISE GLOBALE ET RESTRUCTURATION EUROPÉENNE
Guido La Barbera	LA NOUVELLE PHASE STRATÉGIQUE
Guido La Barbera	LOTTA COMUNISTA – LE GROUPE D'ORIGINE, 1943-1952
Guido La Barbera	LOTTA COMUNISTA – VERS LE PARTI STRATÉGIE, 1953-1965
Guido La Barbera	LOTTA COMUNISTA - LE MODÈLE BOLCHEVIQUE, 1965-1995
Renato Pastorino	LA TÂCHE INÉDITE
Nicola Capelluto	LA CRISE DES RELATIONS GLOBALES
Paolo Rivetti	LES SYNDICATS DANS LA RESTRUCTURATION EUROPÉENNE (2008-2015) et en annexe: Considérations sur les luttes politiques en France (2006-2012)

En partenariat avec éditions L'INTERNATIONALISTE
TERRORISME RÉACTIONNAIRE, EUROPÉISME IMPÉRIALISTE, INTERNATIONALISME COMMUNISTE

Collection Classiques

Karl Marx - Friedrich Engels MANIFESTE DU PARTI COMMUNISTE
En appendice notes sur les premières éditions du Manifeste et sur sa diffusion
Lev Trotsky LES GUERRES BALKANIQUES 1912-1913
Friedrich Engels NOTES SUR LA GUERRE FRANCO-ALLEMANDE DE 1870-1871 Préface de Lev Trotsky

Collection Analyses

Nicola Capelluto - Franco Palumberi
ÉNERGIE ET PÉTROLE DANS L'AFFRONTEMENT IMPÉRIALISTE
Roberto Casella LE SIÈCLE DES GÉANTS DE L'ASIE – I. LA CHINE (1995-2012)
Roberto Casella LE SIÈCLE DES GÉANTS DE L'ASIE – II. L'INDE (1998-2012)
Gianluca De Simone GRAND MOYEN-ORIENT
Crises et guerres de la nouvelle phase stratégique
Giulio Motosi - Piero Nardini LA BATAILLE MONDIALE DE L'ACIER

Collection Documents

G. Munis LEÇONS D'UNE DÉFAITE, PROMESSE DE VICTOIRE
Critique et théorie de la révolution espagnole 1930-1939
Paul Frölich AUTOBIOGRAPHIE
Parcours d'un militant internationaliste allemand : de la social-démocratie au Parti communiste 1890-1921
Paul Frölich, Rudolf Lindau, Albert Schreiner, Jacob Walcher
RÉVOLUTION ET CONTRE-RÉVOLUTION EN ALLEMAGNE 1918-1920
De la fondation du Parti communiste au putsch de Kapp
Paul Frölich IMPÉRIALISME, GUERRE ET LUTTE DE CLASSES EN ALLEMAGNE 1914-1918
Anthologie MARX Scientifique et révolutionnaire
Anthologie LÉNINE Conscience et volonté révolutionnaires
Anthologie ENGELS Science et passion révolutionnaires
G. G. Cavicchioli (Sous la direction de)
OCTOBRE 1917 100 ans, 100 militants de la révolution

bibliothèque jeunes

Lénine	QUE FAIRE ?
	Cervetto – La lutte décisive
Lénine	L'IMPÉRIALISME, STADE SUPRÊME DU CAPITALISME
	Cervetto – La théorie marxiste des relations internationals
Lénine	L'ÉTAT ET LA RÉVOLUTION
	Cervetto – La restauration de la théorie marxiste
Lénine	LA MALADIE INFANTILE DU COMMUNISME (LE « COMMUNISME DE GAUCHE »)
	Cervetto – Le temps de la clarté de Lénine
Lénine	MATÉRIALISME ET EMPIRIOCRITICISME Notes critiques sur une philosophie réactionnaire
	Cervetto – La critique libérale de Bernstein
Lénine	CE QUE SONT LES « AMIS DU PEUPLE » suivi de LE CONTENU ÉCONOMIQUE DU POPULISME
	Cervetto – La théorie de la politique de Lénine
Lénine	LE SOCIALISME ET LA GUERRE
Lénine	LA RÉVOLUTION PROLÉTARIENNE ET LE RÉNÉGAT KAUTSKY
	Cervetto – Le fondement scientifique de la lutte des classes
Cervetto	LÉNINE ET LA RÉVOLUTION CHINOISE
	Lénine – « Matières inflammables de la politique mondiale » et autres écrits
Engels	ANTIDÜHRING
	Cervetto – La découverte de la politique
Engels	LA SITUATION DE LA CLASSE OUVRIÈRE EN ANGLETERRE
	Cervetto – La vision historique de la transformation sociale
Engels	SOCIALISME UTOPIQUE ET SOCIALISME SCIENTIFIQUE suivi de LUDWIG FEUERBACH ET L'ABOUTISSEMENT DE LA PHILOSOPHIE CLASSIQUE ALLEMANDE
Marx - Engels	LA CONCEPTION MATÉRIALISTE DE L'HISTOIRE
Marx	LA GUERRE CIVILE EN FRANCE
Marx	CRITIQUE DE L'ÉCONOMIE POLITIQUE

Marx	TRAVAIL SALARIÉ ET CAPITAL suivi de SALAIRE, PRIX ET PROFIT
Marx	LES LUTTES DE CLASSES EN FRANCE 1848-1850 suivi de LE 18 BRUMAIRE DE LOUIS BONAPARTE
Marx - Engels - Lénine	UNE CAUSE DE L'HUMANITÉ TOUT ENTIÈRE Anthologie
Anthologie	LE CHOIX COMMUNISTE Comprendre le présent, changer l'avenir

Spanish

Textos

Arrigo Cervetto	LUCHA DE CLASES Y PARTIDO REVOLUCIONARIO
Arrigo Cervetto	LA DIFÍCIL CUESTIÓN DE LOS TIEMPOS
Guido La Barbera	LOTTA COMUNISTA – EL GRUPO ORIGINARIO 1943-1952
Guido La Barbera	LOTTA COMUNISTA - HACIA EL PARTIDO ESTRATEGIA 1953-1965
Guido La Barbera	LOTTA COMUNISTA - EL MODEL BOLCHEVIQUE 1965-1995
Guido La Barbera	LA NUEVA FASE ESTRATEGICA
Antologia	TERRORISMO REACCIONARIO EUROPEÍSMO IMPERIALISTA INTERNACIONALISMO COMUNISTA

Documentos

G. G. Cavicchioli (A cargo de)	OCTUBRE DE 1917, 100 AÑOS, 100 MILITANTES DE LA REVOLUCIÓN

Análisis

G. De Simone	GRAN ORIENTE MEDIO Crisis y guerras de la nueva fase estratégica

biblioteca jóvenes

Marx	TRABAJO ASALARIADO Y CAPITAL SALARIO, PRECIO Y GANACIA
Engels	ANTIDÜHRING

Lenin	EL IMPERIALISMO FASE SUPERIOR DEL CAPITALISMO (Esbozo popular) Cervetto - La teoría marxista de las relaciones internacionales
Lenin	EL ESTADO Y LA REVOLUCIÓN Cervetto - La restauración de la teoría marxista
Cervetto	LENIN Y LA REVOLUCIÓN CHINA Lenin - "Material inflamable en la política mundial" y otros escritos
Antologia	LA ELECCIÓN COMUNISTA Comprender el presente, cambiar el futuro
Antologia	NUESTRA LUCHA INTERNACIONALISTA Orientaciones para la nueva fase estratégica

German

Arrigo Cervetto	KLASSENKÄMPFE UND REVOLUTIONÄRE PARTEI
Arrigo Cervetto	DIE POLITISCHE HÜLLE
Anthologie	UNSER INTERNATIONALISTISCHER KAMPF Richtlinien für die neue strategische Phase

Russian books

(Éditions Science Marxiste in collaboration with Prometey Publications, St. Petersburg)

Arrigo Cervetto	UNITARNII IMPERIALISM, TOM I
Arrigo Cervetto	UNITARNII IMPERIALISM, TOM II
Arrigo Cervetto	MNOGOPOLIARNI MIR 1990-1995

NOVY PROMETEY Publications, St. Petersburg, Russia

Arrigo Cervetto	TRUDNIY VOPROS VREMENI
Arrigo Cervetto	POLITIČESKAYA OBOLOČKA
Arrigo Cervetto	METOD E PARTIA-NAUKA
Arrigo Cervetto	KLASSOVAIA BOR'BÁ I REVOLIUTSIONNAIA PARTIA
Guido La Barbera	LOTTA COMUNISTA : GRUPPA, STOYAVSCAYA U ISTOKOV (1943-1952). Appendix: Arrigo Cervetto's political biography and Bukharin's work "Theory of the Imperialist State"
Guido La Barbera	LOTTA COMUNISTA: V NAPRAVLENII PARTII STRATEGII (1953-1965)
Guido La Barbera	NOVAYA STRATEGICHESKAYA FAZA
Renato Pastorino	BESPRETSEDENTNAYA ZADACHA
Gianluca De Simone	BOLSHOY SREDNIY VOSTOK. Krizisy i voyny novoy strategicheskoy fazy
Vladimir Nevskiy	ISTORA RKP(B). KRATIJ OCHERK
Lev Trotsky	BALKANI I BALKANSKAYA VOJNA. Pered istoricheskim rubezhom
Ivan Babushkin	RABOČIJ BOL'SHEVIK
Y. M. Steklov	PERVYY INTERNATSIONAL: MEZHDUNARODNOE TOVARISCHESTVO RABOCHIH 1864-1872
G. G. Cavicchioli	OKTYABR 1917 GODA. 100 let. 100 bortsov za revolyutsiyu
Anthology	REAKTSIONNYIY TERRORIZM, IMPERIALISTICHESKIY EVROPEIZM, KOMMUNISTICHESKIY INTERNATSIONALIZM
Anthology	OBRAZOVANIE KOMMUNISTICHESKOGO INTERNAZIONALA. MART 1919 GODA
Anthology	KOMMUNIZM ILI VARVARSTVO ?
Anthology	NAŠA INTERNATSIONALISTIESKAJA BOR'BA. Orientiry dlja novoj strategiÿeskoj fazy

Greek books

DIETHNISMOS (Internationalism) Publications, Piraeus, Greece

Anthology	Ο ΜΥΘΟΣ ΤΟΥ ΚΑΛΠΙΚΟΥ ΣΟΣΙΑΛΙΣΜΟΥ (Le mythe du faux socialisme)
Arrigo Cervetto	ΤΑΞΙΚΟΙ ΑΓΩΝΣ ΚΑΙ ΕΠΑΝΑΣΤΑΤΙΚΟ ΚΟΜΜΑ (Luttes de classe et parti révolutionnaire)
Arrigo Cervetto	ΤΟ ΔΣΚΟΛΟ ΖΗΤΗΜΑ ΤΩΝ ΧΡΟΝΩΝ (La difficile question des temps)
Renato Pastorino	ΤΟ ΠRΩΤΟΓΝΩΡΟ ΚΑΘΗΚΟΝ (La tâche inédite)
Guido La Barbera	Η ΕΥΡΩΠΗ ΚΑΙ Ο ΠΟΛΕΜΟΣ (L'Europe et la guerre)
Anthology	Η ΚΟΜΜΟΎΝΙΣΤΙΚΗ ΕΠΙΛΟΓΗ Να καταλάβουμε το παρόν να αλλάξουμε το μέλλον (Le choix communiste)
Anthology	ΜΙΑ ΥΠΟΘΕΣΗ ΟΛΗΣ ΤΗΣ ΑΝΘΡΩΠΟΤΗΤΑΣ (Une cause de l'humanité tout entière)
Anthology	ΜΥΘΟΙ ΚΑΙ ΠΟΛΕΜΟΙ ΣΤΙΣ ΜΠΑΝΛΙΕ ΤΟΥ ΕΥΡΩΠΑΪΚΟΥ ΙΜΠΕΡΙΑΛΙΣΜΟΥ (Mythes et guerres dans les banlieues de l'impérialisme européen)
Anthology	1991-2011 : 20 ΧΡΟΝΙΑ ΠΟΥ ΑΛΛΑΞΑΝ ΤΟΝ ΚΟΣΜΟ (1991-2011 : 20 années qui ont ébranlé le monde)
Anthology	Η ΕΥΡΩΠΗ-ΔΥΝΜΗ : Ο ΕΧΘΡΟΣ ΣΤΟ ΣΠΙΤΙ ΜΑΣ (L'Europe puissance : l'ennemi est chez nous)
Anthology	Η ΥΛΙΣΤΙΚΗ ΑΝΤΙΛΗΨΗ ΤΗΣ ΙΣΤΟΡΙΑΣ (La conception materialiste de l'histoire)
Anthology	ΧΡΟΝΟΙ ΚΡΙΣΗΣ, ΕΠΙΣΤΡΟΦΗ ΣΤΟΝ ΜΑΡΞ (Années de crise, retour à Marx)
Anthology	ΤΟ ΠΡΩΤΟ ΠΡΑΚΤΙΚΟ ΒΗΜΑ (Le premier pas pratique)

Brazilian books

Edições INTERVENÇÃO COMUNISTA Niterói-RJ. – Brazil

Arrigo Cervetto	LUTAS DE CLASE E PARTIDO REVOLUCIONÁRIO
Arrigo Cervetto	LÊNIN E A REVOLUÇÃO CHINESA Lênin – «Material inflamável na politica mundial » e outros textos
Arrigo Cervetto	A DIFÍCIL QUESTÃO DOS TEMPOS
Arrigo Cervetto	MÉTODO E PARTIDO-CIÊNCIA
Arrigo Cervetto	O INVOLUCRO POLITICO
Guido La Barbera	A NOVA FASE ESTRATÉGICA
Anthology	A ESCOLHA COMUNISTA
Anthology	A ASCENSÃO IMPERIALISTA DO BRASIL Uma análise marxista
Anthology	A NOSSA LUTA INTERNACIONALISTA

Cet ouvrage a été achevé d'imprimer en septembre 2018
par Galli/Thierry Stampa – Milano
Dépôt légal : septembre 2018
Imprimé en Italie